Existentialism: A Very Short Introduction

VERY SHORT INTRODUCTIONS are for anyone wanting a stimulating and accessible way in to a new subject. They are written by experts, and have been published in more than 25 languages worldwide.

The series began in 1995, and now represents a wide variety of topics in history, philosophy, religion, science, and the humanities. Over the next few years it will grow to a library of around 200 volumes – a Very Short Introduction to everything from ancient Egypt and Indian philosophy to conceptual art and cosmology.

Very Short Introductions available now:

For more information visit our web site

www.oup.co.uk/general/vsi/

Thomas Flynn

EXISTENTIALISM

A Very Short Introduction

OXFORD
UNIVERSITY PRESS

OXFORD

UNIVERSITY PRESS

Great Clarendon Street, Oxford OX2 6DP

Oxford University Press is a department of the University of Oxford.
It furthers the University's objective of excellence in research, scholarship,
and education by publishing worldwide in

Oxford New York

Auckland Cape Town Dar es Salaam Hong Kong Karachi
Kuala Lumpur Madrid Melbourne Mexico City Nairobi
New Delhi Shanghai Taipei Toronto

With offices in

Argentina Austria Brazil Chile Czech Republic France Greece
Guatemala Hungary Italy Japan Poland Portugal Singapore
South Korea Switzerland Thailand Turkey Ukraine Vietnam

Oxford is a registered trade mark of Oxford University Press
in the UK and in certain other countries

Published in the United States
by Oxford University Press Inc., New York

© Thomas Flynn 2006

The moral rights of the author have been asserted
Database right Oxford University Press (maker)

First published as a Very Short Introduction 2006

British Library Cataloguing in Publication Data
Data available

Library of Congress Cataloging in Publication Data
Data available

Typeset by RefineCatch Ltd, Bungay, Suffolk
Printed in Great Britain by
Ashford Colour Press Ltd., Gosport, Hants

ISBN 978-0-19-280428-0

5 7 9 10 8 6

Contents

For Rose and Bob Flynn, Brady, Colin, and Alanna

Preface

Existentialism is commonly associated with Left-Bank Parisian cafes and the 'family' of philosophers Jean-Paul Sartre and Simone de Beauvoir who gathered there in the years immediately following the liberation of Paris at the end of World War II. One imagines off-beat, avant-garde intellectuals, attached to their cigarettes, listening to jazz as they hotly debate the implications of their new-found political and artistic liberty. The mood is one of enthusiasm, creativity, anguished self-analysis, and freedom – always freedom.

Though this reflects the image projected by the media of the day and doubtless captures the spirit of the time, it glosses over the philosophical significance of existentialist thought, packaging it as a cultural phenomenon of a certain historical period. That is perhaps the price paid by a manner of thinking so bent on doing philosophy concretely rather than in some abstract and timeless manner. The existentialists' urge for contemporary relevance fired their social and political commitment. But it also linked them with the problems of their day and invited subsequent generations to view them as having the currency of yesterday's news.

Such is the misreading of existentialist thought that I hope to correct in this short volume. If it bears the marks of its post-war appearance, existentialism as a manner of doing philosophy and a way of addressing the issues that matter in people's lives is at least as old as philosophy itself. It is as current as the human condition which it examines. To ensure at the outset that this point is not lost, I begin my initial chapter with a discussion of philosophy, not as a doctrine or a system of thought but as a way of life. The title of Chapter 1 comes from Classical scholar Pierre Hadot's study of the return to the Stoics as an example of how 'Ancient' philosophy can offer meaning to people's lives even in our day. Though his preference is for the Greeks and Romans, Hadot finds a similar concern in the writings of Søren Kierkegaard and Friedrich Nietzsche, the so-called 19th-century 'fathers' of the existentialist movement, and among their 20th-century progeny.

It is commonly acknowledged that existentialism is a philosophy about the concrete individual. This is both its glory and its shame. In an age of mass communication and mass destruction, it is to its credit that existentialism defends the intrinsic value of what its main proponent Sartre calls the 'free organic individual', that is, the flesh-and-blood agent. Because of the almost irresistible pull toward conformity in modern society, what we shall call 'existential individuality' is an achievement, and not a permanent one at that. We are born biological beings but we must become existential individuals by accepting responsibility for our actions. This is an application of Nietzsche's advice to 'become what you are'. Many people never do acknowledge such responsibility but rather flee their existential individuality into the comfort of the faceless crowd. As an object lesson in becoming an individual, in the following chapter, I trace what Kierkegaard calls 'spheres' of existence or 'stages on life's way' and conclude with some observations about how Nietzsche would view this project of becoming an existential individual.

Shortly after the end of the war, Sartre delivered a public lecture entitled 'Is Existentialism a Humanism?' that rocked the intellectual life of Paris and served as a quasi-manifesto for the movement. From then on, existentialism was associated with a certain kind of humanistic philosophy that gives human beings and human values pride of place, and with critiques of alternative versions of humanism accepted at that time. In Chapter 3, I discuss the implications of that problematic lecture, the only one Sartre ever regretted publishing, as well as his contemporary Martin Heidegger's 'response' in his famous *Letter on Humanism*.

While the supreme value of existentialist thought is commonly acknowledged to be freedom, its primary virtue is authenticity. Chapter 4 is devoted to this topic as well as to the nature and forms of self-deception, or bad faith, that function as its contrary. I relate authenticity to existential individuality and consider the possibility of an ethics of authenticity based on existential responsibility.

In order to counter the criticism, widespread immediately after the war, that existentialism is simply another form of bourgeois individualism, bereft of collective consciousness and indifferent to the need to address the social issues of the day, I devote Chapter 5 to the issue of a 'chastened individualism', as the existentialists try to conceive of social solidarity in a manner that will enhance rather than compromise individual freedom and responsibility, which remain non-negotiable.

In the last chapter, I draw on the foregoing as well as on other aspects of existentialist thought to consider the continued relevance of existentialist philosophy in our day. It is necessary to separate the philosophical significance of the movement, its powerful insights, and its attention to the concrete, from the arresting but now dated trappings of its Left-Bank adolescence. From many likely candidates, I choose four topics of current interest to which the existentialists have something of philosophical import to say.

Two features of this brief volume may perhaps strike the reader as limitations even in a short introduction: the number of commonly recognized 'existentialist' names that are absent and, at the other extreme, the possibly excessive presence of Jean-Paul Sartre throughout the work. Regarding the first, though I could have mentioned, for example, Dostoevsky or Kafka, Giacometti or Picasso, Ionesco or Beckett, all powerful exemplars of existentialist themes in the arts, my concern is to treat existentialism as a philosophical movement with artistic implications rather than as (just) a literary movement with philosophical pretensions – which is a common though misguided conception. The reason for not discussing Buber or Berdaiev, Ortega y Gasset or Unamuno, and many other philosophers deserving of mention here, is that this is a 'very' short introduction, after all. Those interested in pursuing the topics discussed here will find suggestions of useful sources at the end of the book.

As for the prominence of Sartre, he and de Beauvoir are the only philosophers in this group who admitted to being existentialists. To the extent that it is a 20th-century movement, existentialism certainly centred on his work. And no one better exemplifies the union of and tension between philosophy and literature, the conceptual and the imaginary, the critical and the committed, philosophy as reflection and philosophy as way of life, that defines the existentialist mode of philosophizing than does Jean-Paul Sartre.

Acknowledgements

This short volume was written under the ideal conditions provided by the Center for Humanistic Inquiry at Emory University. I am most grateful for the Senior Research Fellowship as well as for the support of Tina Brownley, Steve Everett, Keith Anthony, Amy Erbil, and Collette Barlow of the Center in making this possible and bringing it to completion.

I appreciate the comments of David Carr, Tony Jensen, Vanessa Rumble, and Cindy Willett on specific portions of the manuscript. The inevitable omissions, oversights, and errors in a short and simple study of an increasingly long and complex subject are clearly my own. My thanks to John Mercer for compiling the index.

Finally, I wish to dedicate this work to my sister, her husband, and their family, whose love remains as authentic as it is human. *Quam bonum et quam iucundum habitare in unum.*

List of illustrations

The publisher and the author apologize for any errors or omissions in the above list. If contacted they will be pleased to rectify these at the earliest opportunity.

Chapter 1
Philosophy as a way of life

If I do not reveal my views on justice in words, I do so by my conduct.

Socrates to Xenophon

Despite its claim to be novel and unprecedented, existentialism represents a long tradition in the history of philosophy in the West, extending back at least to Socrates (469–399 BC). This is the practice of philosophy as 'care of the self' (*epimeleia heautou*). Its focus is on the proper way of acting rather than on an abstract set of theoretical truths. Thus the Athenian general Laches, in a Platonic dialogue by that name, admits that what impresses him about Socrates is not his teaching but the harmony between his teaching and his life. And Socrates himself warns the Athenian court at the trial for his life that they will not easily find another like him who will instruct them to care for their selves above all else.

This concept of philosophy flourished among the Stoic and Epicurean philosophers of the Hellenistic period. Their attention was focused primarily on ethical questions and discerning the proper way to live one's life. As one Classical scholar put it, 'Philosophy among the Greeks was more formative than informative in nature'. The philosopher was a kind of doctor of the soul, prescribing the proper attitudes and practices to foster health and happiness.

Of course, philosophy as the pursuit of basic truths about human nature and the universe was also widespread among the Ancient Greeks and was an ingredient in the care of the self. It was this more theoretical approach that led to the rise of science and came to dominate the teaching of philosophy in the medieval and modern periods. Indeed, 'theory' today is commonly taken as synonymous with 'philosophy' in general, as in the expressions 'political theory' and 'literary theory', to such an extent that 'theoretical philosophy' is almost redundant.

At issue in this distinction between two forms of philosophy (among other things) are two different uses of 'truth': the scientific and the moral. The former is more cognitive and theoretical, the latter more self-formative and practical, as in 'to thine own self be true'. Whereas the former made no demands on the kind of person one should become in order to know the truth (for the 17th-century philosopher René Descartes, a sinner could grasp a mathematical formula as fully as a saint), the latter kind of truth required a certain self-discipline, a set of practices on the self such as attention to diet, control of one's speech, and regular meditation, in order to be able to access it. It was a matter of becoming a certain kind of person, the way Socrates exhibited a particular way of life, rather than of achieving a certain clarity of argument or insight in the way Aristotle did. In the history of philosophy, care of the self was gradually marginalized and consigned to the domains of spiritual direction, political formation, and psychological counselling. There were important exceptions to this exiling of 'moral' truth from the academy. St Augustine's *Confessions* (AD 397), Blaise Pascal's *Pensées* (1669), and the writings of the German Romantics in the early 19th century are examples of works that encouraged this understanding of philosophy as care of the self.

It is in this larger tradition that existentialism as a philosophical movement can be located. The existentialists can be viewed as reviving this more personal notion of 'truth', a truth that is lived as distinct from and often in opposition to the more detached and scientific use of the term.

It is not surprising that both Søren Kierkegaard (1813–55) and Friedrich Nietzsche (1844–1900), the 19th-century 'fathers of existentialism', had ambivalent attitudes towards the philosophy of Socrates. On the one hand, he was seen as the defender of a kind of rationality that moved beyond merely conventional and subjective values towards universal moral norms, for which Kierkegaard praised him and Nietzsche censured him. But they both respected his individuating 'leap' across the gap in rationality between the proofs of personal immortality and his choice to accept the sentence of death imposed by the Athenian court. (Socrates was tried and found guilty on charges of impiety and for corrupting the youth by his teaching.) In other words, each philosopher realized that life does not follow the continuous flow of logical argument and that one often has to risk moving beyond the limits of the rational in order to live life to the fullest. As Kierkegaard remarked, many people have offered proofs for the immortality of the soul, but Socrates, after hypothesizing that the soul *might* be immortal, risked his life with that possibility in mind. He drank the poison as commanded by the Athenian court, all the while discoursing with his followers on the possibility that another life *may* await him. Kierkegaard called this an example of 'truth as subjectivity'. By this he meant a personal conviction on which one is willing to risk one's life. In his *Journals*, Kierkegaard muses: 'the thing is to find a truth which is true *for me*, to find the idea for which I can live and die' (1 August 1835).

Clarity is not enough

Galileo wrote that the book of nature was written in mathematical characters. Subsequent advances in modern science seemed to confirm this claim. It appeared that whatever could be weighed and measured (quantified) could give us reliable knowledge, whereas the non-measurable was left to the realm of mere opinion. This view became canonized by positivist philosophy in the 19th and early 20th centuries. This positivist habit of mind insisted that the 'objective' was synonymous with the measurable and the 'value-free'. Its aim was to extract the subject from the experiment in order to obtain a purely impersonal 'view from nowhere'. This led to a number of significant discoveries, but it quickly became apparent that such an approach was inconsistent. The limiting of the knowable to the quantifiable was itself a value that was not quantifiable. That is, the choice of this procedure was itself a 'leap' of sorts, an act of faith in a certain set of values that were not themselves measurable.

Moreover, the exclusion of the non-measurable from what counted as knowledge left some of our most important questions not only unanswered but unanswerable. Are our ethical rules and values merely the expression of our subjective preferences? To paraphrase the mathematician and philosopher Bertrand Russell, scarcely an existentialist: can anyone really believe that the revulsion they feel when they witness the gratuitous infliction of pain is simply an expression of the fact that they don't happen to like it? Such was the doctrine of the 'emotivists' in ethical theory, sometimes called the 'boo/hurrah' theory of moral judgements. They were forced in that direction by acceptance of the positivist limitation of knowledge to the measurable. But are we even capable of the kind of antiseptic knowledge that the positivists require of science? Perhaps the knowing subject can be reintroduced into these discussions without compromising their objectivity. Much will depend on us revising our definition of 'objectivity' as well as on discovering other uses of the word 'true' besides the positivists' 'agreement with sense experience'. The existentialists among others responded to this challenge.

Jean-Paul Sartre (1905–80) exemplifies this response when he remarks that the only theory of knowledge that can be valid today is one which is founded on that truth of microphysics: the experimenter is part of the experimental system. What he has in mind is the so-called Heisenberg Uncertainty Principle from atomic physics which, in its popular interpretation at least, states that the instruments which enable us to observe the momentum and the position of an orbital electron interfere with the process such that we can determine the one or the other but never both at once. Analogously, one can object that the very act of intervening in the life of a 'primitive' tribe prevents the ethnologist from studying that people in their pristine condition. Such considerations served to undermine the positivists' concept of knowledge as measurability. But they also clouded the rationalists' view of reality as exhaustively available to a logic of either/or with no middle ground. To cite another example, light manifests qualities that indicate it is a wave and others that show it to be a particle. Yet these two characteristics seem to exclude each other, leaving the question 'Is light a wave or a particle?' unanswerable with the standard logic of either/or. Light seems to be both and yet neither exclusively. Another kind of logic seems called for to make sense of this phenomenon. Numerous other examples from physics and mathematics appeared early in the last century that offered counterexamples to the positivists' and the rationalists' claims about knowledge and the world.

Lived experience

It is into this world of limited and relative observation and assessment that the existentialist enters with his/her drive to 'personalize' the most impersonal phenomena in our lives. What, for example, could be more impersonal and objective than space and time? Even the chastened view of space-time that the Relativity Theory offers us relies on an absolute or constant referent, namely the speed of light. We measure time by minutes and seconds and chart space by yards or metres. This too seems quantitative and hence objective in the positivists' sense. And yet the notion of what existentialists call 'ekstatic' temporality adds a qualitative and personal dimension to the phenomenon of time-consciousness. For the existentialist, the value and meaning of each temporal dimension of lived time is a function of our attitudes and choices. Some people, for example, are always pressed to meet obligations whereas others are at a loss to occupy their time. Time rushes by when you're having fun and hangs heavy on your hands when you are in pain. Even the quantitative advice to budget our time, from an existentialist point of view, is really a recommendation to examine and assess the life decisions that establish our temporal priorities in the first place. If 'time is of the essence', and the existentialist will insist that it is, then part of who we are is our manner of living the 'already' and the 'not yet' of our existence, made concrete by how we handle our immersion in the everyday.

The existentialist often dramatizes such 'lived time'. Thus, Albert Camus (1913–60) in his allegory of the Nazi occupation of Paris, *The Plague*, describes the people in a plague-ridden, quarantined city: 'Hostile to the past, impatient of the present, and cheated of the future, we were much like those whom men's justice, or hatred, forces to live behind prison bars.' The notion of imprisonment as 'doing time' is clearly existential. And Sartre, in an insightful analysis of emotive consciousness, speaks of someone literally 'jumping for joy' as a way of using their bodily changes to conjure up, as if by magic, the possibility of possessing a desirable situation 'all at once' without having to await its necessary, temporal unfolding. Though Sartre stated this thesis in the 1930s, one immediately thinks of the photo of Hitler's little 'jig' under the Arc de Triomphe during the German occupation of Paris. Time has its own viscosity, as Michel Foucault remarked. Ekstatic temporality embodies its flow.

But existential space is personalized as well. Sartre cites the social psychologist Kurt Lewin's notion of 'hodological' space (lived space) as the qualitative equivalent to the lived time of our quotidian existence. The story is told of two people, one who prefers to get as closely face-to-face in conversation as possible and the other a distant, stand-off kind of person, propelling and repelling each other around the room at a cocktail party in an attempt to carry on a conversation. Lived space is personal; it is the usual route I take to work, the seating arrangement that quickly establishes itself in a classroom, or the ordering of the objects on my desk. It is what psychologists call my 'comfort zone'. This too is a function of my life project. How I deal with my meaningful 'spaces' depends on how I choose to order my life.

These are, of course, psychological considerations. But it is a defining feature of existentialist thought and method that they carry an ontological significance as well. They articulate our ways of existing and provide access to the meaning and direction (two translations of the French word '*sens*') of our lives. As we shall see, whereas many philosophers have tended to discount or even to criticize the philosophical significance of our feelings and emotions, the existentialists will place great significance on such emotions as 'anguish' (which Kierkegaard called our awareness of our freedom) and feelings like 'nausea' (which Sartre characterized as our experience of the contingency of existence and a 'phenomenon of being'). This sets them immediately in likely dialogue with creative artists, who trade on our emotional and imaginative lives. In fact, the relation between existentialism and the fine arts has been so close that its critics have often dismissed it as solely a literary movement. To be sure, the dramatic nature of existentialist thought, as well as its respect for the disclosing power of emotional consciousness and its use of 'indirect communication', to be discussed shortly, does invite the association. But the issues they address, the careful distinctions they draw, their rigorous descriptions, and, above all, their explicit conversation with others in the philosophical tradition clearly identify the existentialists as primarily philosophical even as they underscore the ambiguity of the distinction between the conceptual and the imaginative, the philosophical and the literary.

'A truth to die for'

If impersonal space and time can be personalized and brought into the domain of our choice and responsibility, so too can the notion of 'objective' truth. As mentioned at the outset, Kierkegaard

Five themes of existentialism

There are five basic themes that the existentialist appropriates each in his or her own way. Rather than constituting a strict definition of 'existentialist', they depict more of a family resemblance (a criss-crossing and overlapping of the themes) among these philosophers.

1. *Existence precedes essence*. What you are (your essence) is the result of your choices (your existence) rather than the reverse. Essence is not destiny. You are what you make yourself to be.

2. *Time is of the essence*. We are fundamentally time-bound beings. Unlike measurable, 'clock' time, lived time is qualitative: the 'not yet', the 'already', and the 'present' differ among themselves in meaning and value.

3. *Humanism*. Existentialism is a person-centred philosophy. Though not anti-science, its focus is on the human individual's pursuit of identity and meaning amidst the social and economic pressures of mass society for superficiality and conformism.

4. *Freedom/responsibility*. Existentialism is a philosophy of freedom. Its basis is the fact that we can stand back from our lives and reflect on what we have been doing. In this sense, we are always 'more' than ourselves. But we are as responsible as we are free.

5. *Ethical considerations are paramount*. Though each existentialist understands the ethical, as with 'freedom', in his or her own way, the underlying concern is to invite us to examine the authenticity of our personal lives and of our society.

distinguished between 'objective' and 'subjective' reflection and truth. He allowed for the common scientific uses of objective reflection, which he described as follows:

> The way of objective reflection makes the subject accidental, and thereby transforms existence into something indifferent, something vanishing. Away from the subject the objective way of reflection leads to the objective truth, and while the subject and his subjectivity become indifferent, the truth also becomes indifferent, and this indifference is precisely its objective validity; for all interest, like all decisiveness, is rooted in subjectivity. The way of objective reflection leads to abstract thought, to mathematics, to historical knowledge of different kinds; and always it leads away from the subject, whose existence or non-existence, and rightly so, becomes infinitely indifferent.

The existentialists are not irrationalists in the sense that they deny the validity of logical argument and scientific reasoning. They simply question the ability of such reasoning to access the deep personal convictions that guide our lives. As Kierkegaard said of the dialectical rationalism of Hegel: 'Trying to live your life by this abstract philosophy is like trying to find your way around Denmark with a map on which that country appears the size of a pinhead.'

In contrast to the objective reflection that ignores individual existence, Kierkegaard speaks of subjective reflection and its corresponding truth as subjectivity:

> When subjectivity is truth, subjectivity's definition must include an expression for an opposition to objectivity, a reminder of the fork in the road, and this expression must also convey the tension of inwardness [the self's relation to itself]. Here is such a definition of truth: *the objective uncertainty, held fast in an appropriation process of the most passionate inwardness is the truth*, the highest truth available for an *existing* person.

Here too it is a matter of a change in the direction one is taking in one's life, the 'fork in the road'. That is what makes the option for subjective reflection an 'existential' choice. Were it simply a question of an impersonal claim about a fact or a law of nature, we would be dealing with 'objective certainty' and the wager of one's personal existence would be irrelevant. One would simply be following the complete directions. Such would be the case of Socrates if his belief in personal immorality were merely the conclusion of an argument. But here the 'truth' is more of a 'moral' nature. As Kierkegaard says, it's a question of 'appropriation' (of 'making it one's own') rather than of 'approximation' to some objective state of affairs, the way one weighs the probabilities of a possible outcome or reads the distance markers along the way to a destination. As he notes elsewhere, for truth as subjectivity, the emphasis is on the 'how' and not on the 'what' of our belief. This has led some to misunderstand him as claiming that it doesn't matter what you believe so long as you believe it. Though scarcely espousing religious relativism, as a deeply committed Christian, Kierkegaard was more concerned with combating lukewarm or purely nominal religious belief than with apologetics.

If one translates a secularized existential truth into the language of the meaning of life, it would imply that there is no 'objectively' correct path to choose. Rather, for the existentialist, after getting clear on the options and the likely outcomes, one *makes* it the right choice by one's follow-through. For the existentialist, such truth is more a matter of decision than of discovery. But, of course, one is not making these choices blindly and without criteria (contrary to popular misconception). But the nature of the choice is criterion-*constituting* rather than criterion*less*, as some have objected. What Kierkegaard is talking about expresses what one might call a 'conversion' experience, where the decisive move is not purely intellectual but a matter of will and feeling (what Kierkegaard calls 'passion') as well. Such is the nature of the so-called 'blind leap' of faith that catapults one into the religious sphere of existence, as we shall see in the next chapter. But it applies

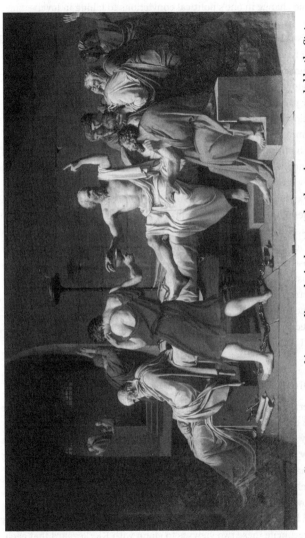

1. Socrates discourses over personal immortality as he is about to take the poison as commanded by the State

equally to other fundamental 'turnings' in a person's life, from a basic change in one's political convictions to falling in love.

This is but one of many places where existentialist, pragmatist, and 'analytic' philosophy overlap. The great American psychologist and pragmatist philosopher William James, for instance, makes an analogous claim in his *The Will To Believe* when he observes that our passional nature not only lawfully may, but must, decide an option between propositions, whenever it is a genuine option that cannot by its nature be decided on intellectual grounds. But some such options are what British ethicist R. M. Hare calls 'decisions of principle'. Such decisions are not themselves principled because they are what establish the principles according to which we shall make subsequent options in our life. Such principles are like the 'rules of the game' that one opts for when deciding to participate but which do not apply beforehand. You do not follow those rules before deciding to play the game; your decision to play means abiding by those very rules. These are what I have been calling 'criteria-constituting' choices. As we shall see, this is analogous to what Sartre calls initial or 'fundamental Choice' that gives unity and direction to a person's life. We discover it by reflecting on the direction of our lives up to the present. It is a 'Choice', Sartre claims, that we find we've already made implicitly all along.

Committed philosophy and literature

Kierkegaard's 'truth' as subjectivity is the forerunner to what Sartre will call 'commitment' (*l'engagement*) in the next century. As if to play down the concept of objective truth, or at least to subscribe to a new meaning for 'objectivity' in light of late modern science, Sartre remarks: 'There is only committed knowledge.' On the other hand, he also subscribes to the more classical, 'objectivist' view of knowledge and truth proposed by Edmund Husserl (1859–1938) and his descriptive method of phenomenology (see below). One way to reconcile these two views is to claim with Kierkegaard that each refers to a different use of the term 'truth'. In Sartre's case, it may be a question of absorbing the phenomenological descriptions into a more pragmatist, dialectical notion of truth; that is, one that reconciles alternative claims in a higher viewpoint. This would fit better with a hermeneutical or interpretive phenomenology such as Martin Heidegger (1889–1976) introduced in the 1920s (see Chapter 6). Nietzsche had insisted that all knowledge was interpretation and that there was no 'original' non-interpreted text. In other words, what counted as knowledge was interpretation 'all the way down'. So whether completely with Nietzsche or merely in part with Kierkegaard, truth too has been 'personalized' by the existentialists. 'My truth' ceases to be a self-contradictory expression.

In a famous set of essays, *What is Literature?* published in 1948, Sartre develops the concept of 'committed literature'. His basic premise is that writing is a form of action for which responsibility must be taken, but that this responsibility carries over into the content and not just the form of what is communicated. The experience of the Second World War had given Sartre a sense of social responsibility that, arguably, was lacking or at least ill-developed in his masterpiece, *Being and Nothingness* (1943). In fact, the existentialists had generally been criticized for their excessive individualism and apparent lack of social conscience. Sartre, who had already distinguished himself with several well-received plays and the impressive novel *Nausea*, now addressed the moral responsibility of the prose artist. 'Though literature is one thing and morality another,' he admits, 'at the heart of the aesthetic imperative we discern the moral imperative', namely an act of confidence in the freedom of both parties. The concept of the relation between artist and audience as one of 'gift-appeal' emerges as central to Sartre's aesthetics and soon serves as the model for disalienated social relations generally; that is, the example for relations that do not treat humans as mere things or instruments but as values in themselves. What might appear to be the merely formal condition of one freedom respecting another assumes a substantive character when Sartre concludes:

The unique point of view from which the author can present the world to those freedoms whose concurrence he wishes to bring about is that of a world to be impregnated always with more freedom. It would be inconceivable that this unleashing of generosity provoked by the writer could be used to authorize an injustice, and that the reader could enjoy his freedom while reading a work which approves or accepts *or simply abstains from condemning* the subjection of man by man.

In other words, as we shall see, existentialism is developing a social conscience and, with it, a conviction that the fine arts, literature at least, should be socially and politically committed.

In this seminal essay, written in the early post-war years, in a remark he will come to regret, Sartre draws a famous distinction between poetry and prose. Poetry, on this account, signifies any non-instrumentalist form of language or of any art form such as music and visual and plastic art. Such forms essentially pursue art for its own sake and so are incapable of commitment to social change under pain of violating their artistic nature. Prose, on the other hand, because it is instrumental in character, can and, in our day, should be committed to the fostering of individual and collective freedom both by the subject matter it addresses and by its manner of treatment. Though he will subsequently revise that distinction in an essay on the revolutionary character of Black African Francophone poetry, Sartre's general thesis remains that literature, at least in our current situation of what he sees as social oppression and economic exploitation, should be committed to its alleviation. As he wrote, merely failing to condemn such practices is not enough. Active opposition is called for. We shall pursue the matter of social responsibility among the various existentialist authors in Chapter 5. But for the moment it may suffice to mention the socially and politically 'committed' character of the artistic works that several of these writers produced.

2. Sartre addresses a student uprising in 1968

Jean-Paul Sartre (1905–80)

A native Parisian, he was probably the most renowned philosopher of the 20th century. He travelled extensively throughout the world, usually with his lifelong partner, Simone de Beauvoir. His name became synonymous with the existentialist movement. He wrote numerous plays, novels, and philosophical works, the most famous of which was *Being and Nothingness* (1943). Offered the Nobel Prize for Literature, he declined the honour. He was deeply committed to the political Left for the greater part of his public life. At his death, thousands of people spontaneously filled the streets to join his cortège. As one publication headlined: 'France has lost its conscience.'

Existentialism and the fine arts: indirect communication

Because of its dramatic conception of existence, its widespread use of powerful images in its arguments, and its appeal to personal response in its communications, existentialism has always been closely associated with the fine arts. In fact, both Camus and Sartre were offered the Nobel Prize for Literature (which Sartre declined). Kierkegaard was a kind of poet who used pseudonyms, parables, and other forms of 'indirect communication' to enlist our personal involvement in the matter at hand. Nietzsche was one of the great prose artists of the German language and his allegory of a religious prophet, *Thus Spoke Zarathustra*, like Sartre's *Nausea*, is a model of philosophical dramatization. The novels of Simone de Beauvoir (1908–86), too, are expressions of her philosophical insights. Gabriel Marcel (1889–1973) wrote philosophy in a meditative manner that he once said was perhaps better exhibited in his 30 published plays. Among the philosophers we are discussing, perhaps only Heidegger, Karl Jaspers (1883–1969), and Maurice Merleau-Ponty (1908–61) fit least appropriately in this category. Yet, with the exception of Jaspers, even they wrote significant studies in aesthetics and all three employed the phenomenological method that valorizes argument by example. Each insisted that the artist, especially the poet in Heidegger's case, and the visual artist for Merleau-Ponty, anticipates and often more adequately expresses what the philosopher is trying to conceptualize. So strong is the influence of existentialist ideas in the fine arts that, as we have seen, some would prefer to describe existentialism as a literary movement. Certainly, authors like Dostoevsky and Kafka, playwrights like Beckett and Ionesco, and artists like Giacometti and Picasso exemplify many of the defining characteristics of existentialist thought.

The concept of commitment to social and moral reform that characterizes all of these writers finds its most apt expression in what came to be called their use of 'indirect communication' to transmit their ideas. The term denotes a rhetorical move that conceals the philosopher's authorial identity in order to invite the reader's identification with the characters of the work by suspension of their disbelief. Thus Kierkegaard could write in the voices of different pseudonymous authors, each conveying a certain viewpoint associated with that persona and not precisely with the philosopher himself. Nietzsche was able to parody scriptural prophecy even as he undermined religious belief in his *Thus Spoke Zarathustra*. Even his aphorisms, though enunciated in his own name, carry the rhetorical force of a blow to the head, despite one's occasional misgivings about where it came from, that is, what kind of 'argument' stands behind it. Similarly, de Beauvoir, Sartre, Camus, and Marcel could write novels and plays that conveyed their ideas in concrete fashion to an audience that, for the moment at least, had suspended its critical distance. Once asked why he presented his plays in the bourgeois quarters of the city rather than in its working-class sections, Sartre replied that no bourgeois could witness a performance of one of his plays without having entertained thoughts 'traitorous to his class'. Such is the power of art to convey a philosophical invitation to a way of life.

Husserl and the phenomenological method

Though the phenomenological method developed by Edmund Husserl in the first third of the 20th century was adopted in one form or another by the existentialists of that same period, many, perhaps most, phenomenologists are not existentialists. But all accept the best-known and most significant claim of this approach, namely that all consciousness is consciousness *of* an other-than-consciousness. In other words, it is the very nature of consciousness to aim towards (to 'intend') an other. Even when it is directed towards itself in reflection, consciousness is directed as towards an 'other'. This is called the principle of intentionality. In this context, 'intentional' has nothing to do with 'on purpose'. It is a technical term for what is unique about our mental acts: they extend beyond themselves towards an other.

3. **Edmund Husserl, founder of the phenomenological movement**

Edmund Husserl (1859–1938)

Born in Prossnitz, in the Czech Republic, he earned a doctorate in mathematics before turning to philosophy. He taught in Göttingen in Germany from 1901 to 1916, and in Freiburg im Breisgau from 1916 until his retirement in 1928. The founder of phenomenology, Husserl played a seminal role in European philosophy in the 20th century. Martin Heidegger was his most famous pupil and succeeded him at Freiburg. Of Jewish origin, his last years were marred by the rise of National Socialism. At his death in Freiburg, a Belgian priest friend transported his widow and his manuscripts to the University of Louvain before they could be destroyed by the Nazis.

The significance of this principle is twofold. It overcomes the problem of the 'bridge' between ideas 'in' the mind and the external world which they are supposed to resemble. We have no 'third eye' to compare what's in the mind with what's outside so as to confirm our claim to know the external world. This problem was the legacy of the father of modern philosophy, René Descartes (1596–1650), and his followers. In his quest for certitude against sceptical doubt, Descartes concluded that he could be certain of one thing, namely that he was a thinker since doubting was a form of thinking. This seemed to justify his intuitive claim: 'I think therefore I am' (*Cogito ergo sum*). But this hard-won certitude was a Pyrrhic victory, for it left him trapped 'inside' his mind, facing the problem of 'bridging' the gap between inner and outer reality. How could he extend this certainty to the 'external' world?

According to the principle of intentionality, this was a false problem, for there is no inside/outside for consciousness. Every conscious act 'intends' (is intentionally related to) an object that is already 'in' the world. Our manner of 'intending' these objects will differ as we perceive, conceive, imagine, or recollect them, for example, or are related to them in an emotive manner. But in every case, being conscious is a way of being in the world.

Consider our images, for example. As Sartre pointed out in an early study, images are not miniatures 'in the mind' to be projected onto the external world, raising the problem of the correspondence between the inner and the outer once more. Rather, imaging consciousness is a way of 'derealizing' the world of our perceptions that manifests its distinctive features to careful phenomenological description. If we imagine an apple that we previously perceived, for instance, a careful description of the experience will reveal how the imagining differs from the perceiving of the same apple. For one thing, unlike the perceived apple, the imagined one has only those features that we choose to give it. Images as such teach us nothing. And so it is with our other conscious acts. Each reveals its distinctive features to phenomenological description.

But because consciousness 'intends' its objects in such different ways, we can employ the method of phenomenological description called 'eidetic reduction' or the 'free imaginative variation of examples' to arrive at the intelligible contour or essence of any of these diverse conscious experiences. And this imaginative task of rigorous description of what is 'given' to consciousness in its various modes of 'givenness' is what the existentialists favour in mounting their concrete arguments. As Husserl once said, the point of phenomenological method is not to explain (by finding causes) but to get us to see (by presenting essences or intelligible contours).

Consider a couple of examples. A forensic artist might sketch an image of a criminal for an eyewitness to identify. As she adds or subtracts aspects of the image, the witness will agree or disagree with the likeness until, optimally, the person says 'yes, that's the fellow; that's what he looked like'. This is a homely analogy of an eidetic description that uses the free imaginative variation of examples to achieve an insight, an immediate grasp of the object intended.

Let us take for our second example a famous phenomenological 'argument' from Sartre's *Being and Nothingness*, which I take to be a less technical form of eidetic reduction. A voyeur is looking through a keyhole at a couple when suddenly he hears what he takes to be footsteps behind him. In one and the same act, he experiences his body 'objectified' by another consciousness. His mounting embarrassment, his reddening face, is the equivalent of a twofold argument for the existence of other minds (an old philosophical conundrum) and for his body as vulnerable to objectification in a manner over which he has no control. Even if the voyeur were mistaken (the sound was made by the wind in the curtains before the open window), still the experience has justified our belief in other minds far more immediately and with a greater degree of certainty than any argument from analogy, which is the standard empiricist's proof. This is the force of a successful 'eidetic reduction'. It captures the essence or intelligible contour of the experience of another subject as subject and not simply as an object.

The strength and potential weakness of such arguments from phenomenological description or the free imaginative variation of examples is that they home in on what I have been calling an 'intelligible contour'. This is a kind of immediate grasp of the presence of the 'thing itself', as Husserl said. It resembles the 'aha!' experience at the end of a mathematical or logical demonstration (Husserl's doctorate was in mathematics). The assumption is that if the description is mounted rigorously, the inquirer will simply see for himself. The potential weakness, of course, is that, in response to the claim 'I don't see it', the phenomenologist can merely reply, 'well, look more closely'. But, in fact, we often do get the point; we succeed in seeing the invariant 'essence' through the numerous variations. And such arguments by example not only provide the existentialist with the concrete way of reasoning that he is seeking, they almost beg for embodiment in imaginative literature, films, and plays.

I mentioned that many phenomenologists are not existentialists. The converse is also true: while 20th-century existentialists accepted Husserl's concept of intentionality because it opened a wide field for their descriptive method, they resisted another feature of his later thought as being incompatible with what existentialism is all about, namely his project of 'bracketing' existence. Husserl spoke of the natural attitude, which might be described as pre-philosophical and naive in its uncritical acceptance of the real world of everyday experience. In his drive to make phenomenology a strict science synonymous with philosophy itself, Husserl insisted that one should suspend the naive realism of the natural attitude and disregard, or bracket, the question of the existence or being of the objects of phenomenological description. Husserl called this a 'phenomenological reduction', or *epochē*, and he thought it could short-circuit sceptical objections to which the natural attitude was liable. He admitted that one could perform an 'eidetic reduction' in the natural attitude and achieve a kind of 'eidetic' psychology. But he later argued that this left unresolved the sceptical question, 'Does what you're describing hold true in the real world?' Husserl's point was that if you produce this additional reduction and bracket the 'being question' of the objects of your inquiry (setting aside the question whether they exist 'in reality' or merely 'in the mind'), you disarm the sceptic who doubts you can ever attain 'reality' with your descriptions. The point of the phenomenological reduction is to leave everything as grist for the phenomenologist's mill *except* the being of the 'reduced' objects, now called 'phenomena'. When you suspend the being question, you retain all of the experiences and their respective objects that you had before (perceptions, images, memories, and the rest), but now as consciousness-relative, that is, as phenomena. In a sense, you have the same tune as in the natural attitude but now in a different key. Inoculated against sceptical doubt – which has been a negative force driving philosophy since the Greeks – you can now undertake rigorous descriptive analyses of any phenomenon whatsoever. The descriptions themselves will sort out the difference between an apple that is perceived, for example, and one that is merely imagined. This seems to be an ingenious way of marginalizing the philosophical sceptic and assuring our certain knowledge of the world. That was Husserl's dream.

The existentialists offer two reasons for rejecting Husserl's phenomenological reduction. First, it makes our basic relationship to the world theoretical rather than practical, as if we were born theoreticians and later learned about practice. Husserl's student, Martin Heidegger, on the contrary, insisted that we were originally 'in the world' instrumentally by means of our practical concerns and that philosophy should analyse this 'pre-theoretical' awareness in order to gain access to being. Similarly, Sartre, as we saw, insisted that all knowledge was 'committed'. And Merleau-Ponty spoke of a certain 'operative intentionality' of our lived bodies that interacted with the world prior to our reflective conceptualization. Even Husserl, later in life, seemed to acknowledge these claims by introducing the concept of the 'lifeworld' as the pre-theoretical basis of our theoretical reflection.

But the major existentialist objection is that being itself is not an 'essence' subject to reduction and, as Merleau-Ponty famously phrased it, 'a complete [phenomenological] reduction is impossible' because you cannot 'reduce' the existing 'reducer'. The existing individual is more than his or her 'definition' such as one might hope to capture in a theoretical concept. As Sartre argues, there are 'phenomena of being', such as our experience of nausea, that reveal that we are and that we need not be (our 'contingency'). But such an experience is not cognitive. Rather, it is a matter of feeling or emotional consciousness – the stuff of arresting descriptions and novels.

Chapter 2
Becoming an individual

No two beings, and no two situations, are really commensurable
with each other.
To become aware of this fact is to undergo a sort of crisis.

Gabriel Marcel

Existentialism is known as an 'individualistic' philosophy. We shall
qualify this view when we consider its social dimension in Chapter
5. But from the outset we should note that, for the existentialist,
being an individual in our mass society is an achievement rather
than a starting point. Again, each existentialist will treat this
subject in his or her own way. But their underlying theme is that the
pull in modern society is away from individualism and towards
conformity. It is in this respect that Kierkegaard refers to the 'plebs',
Nietzsche unflatteringly speaks of the 'herd', Heidegger of '*Das
Man*', and Sartre the 'one'. In every case, the reference is to thinking,
acting, dressing, speaking, and so forth as 'they' do. In Leo Tolstoy's
short story *The Death of Ivan Ilyich*, the speaker, a conformist and
social climber, frequently refers to behaving '*comme il faut*'
('properly'), even to the point of using the French phrase preferred
by the better levels of society to which he aspires. In that sense,
becoming an individual is a task to be undertaken and sustained
but perhaps never permanently achieved. As we suggested in
the previous chapter, the time-bound nature of the human

condition requires that existing as an individual is always dynamic and under way, never static and complete. And depending on the circumstances, it may also involve considerable risk.

Nietzsche has spoken eloquently of the loneliness of the individual who has risen above the herd. As is often the case with existentialists, his personal life gave tragic witness to the price often demanded for such nonconformity as he sought in the manner of Socrates to harmonize his life with his teaching. For years, Nietzsche moved around Europe, never remaining in the same place more than a few months, living in rented rooms or as the guest of others, suffering from severe migraines and stomach problems, often having to pay for the publication of his own books, which never reached a large audience during his lifetime. He likened himself to Spinoza, a 17th-century Dutch philosopher of Jewish descent who was excommunicated from the Synagogue for his unorthodox views. One of his aphorisms reads: 'To live alone one must be either a beast or a god, says Aristotle. Leaving out the third case: one must be both – a philosopher.' Insisting that the philosopher must act against the received wisdom of the age, Nietzsche remarks:

> Today ... when only the herd animal is honored ... the concept of 'greatness' entails being noble, wanting to be oneself, being capable of being different, standing alone and having to live independently; and the philosopher will betray something of his own ideal when he posits: 'He shall be the greatest who can be the loneliest, the most hidden, the most deviating, the human being beyond good and evil.'

By these criteria, Søren Kierkegaard was the epitome of the Nietzschean philosopher, though the latter seems to have had only a passing acquaintance with his work. Kierkegaard wrote essays and tracts attacking the three most potent forces of conformity in the Copenhagen of his day, namely the popular press, the State Church, and the reigning philosophy, that of

G. W. F. Hegel (1770–1831), each in the name of the individual. The popular press, in his view, did people's thinking for them, the Church their believing for them, and the Hegelianism their choosing for them, in the sense that it 'mediated' otherwise individualizing choices in some higher, encompassing viewpoint in a process called 'dialectic'. In other words, Hegel's philosophy transformed a challenging 'either/or' into a comfortable 'both-and'. These unfavourable judgements, though made in the name of becoming an individual, isolated Kierkegaard from his society and occasioned considerable backlash from the establishment. Indeed, he was reported to have preferred for the epitaph on his tombstone the simple phrase, 'That Single Individual'. Add to this the famous and seemingly heartless breaking of his engagement to Regine Olsen, ostensibly because he did not wish to inflict his singular vocation on her, as well as his subsequent celibate life, and we have the kind of solitary thinker whom Nietzsche lauds as the true philosopher. And in a sense, as we are about to see, Kierkegaard's ideal knight of faith was also 'beyond good and evil', though not precisely in Nietzsche's use of that famous expression.

Kierkegaard's theory of stages

The most extended analysis of the project of becoming an individual appears in two places, Kierkegaard's *Either/Or* and his *Stages on Life's Way*. Both are examples of his method of oblique communication. Each tells a tale, actually several tales, by pseudonymous authors in order to enable us to see and test the respective morals of these stories on our own lives. Together, their narrative arguments provide a rather complete description of the three spheres of existence that Kierkegaard formulates in order to trace the process of becoming an individual. Though we shall have to modify and nuance this process once it has been laid out, the spheres or stages are three (the aesthetic, the ethical, and the religious). Each stage has its own model as befits a morality tale: Don Juan, among others, for the aesthetic, Socrates, again among others, for the ethical, and Abraham for the religious sphere. These figures convey a concrete, emotional force to the 'argument' as it unfolds. Like the docent in an art gallery, Kierkegaard keeps referring to the model as he enables us to see how it instantiates the quality under discussion. So let us follow this path and encounter its literary and historical characters as we progress on the road towards individuality. As one should expect from an existentialist analysis, each stage or sphere will reveal its own relation to temporality that distinguishes it from the others. Again, time is of the essence.

Perhaps the best way to begin is towards the end, when one of its characters, 'Frater Taciturnus', in a letter to the readers of *Stages on Life's Way* summarizes the stages or spheres as follows:

> There are three existence-spheres, the aesthetic, the ethical, the religious.... The ethical sphere is only a transition sphere and therefore its highest expression is repentance as a negative action. The aesthetic sphere is the sphere of immediacy, the ethical the sphere of requirement (and this requirement is so infinite that the individual always goes bankrupt), the religious the sphere of fulfillment, but please note, not a fulfillment such as when one fills an alms box or a sack with gold, for repentance has specifically created a boundless space and as a consequence the religious contradiction: simultaneously to be out on 70,000 fathoms of water and yet be joyful.

Obviously written from a 'religious' viewpoint, Brother Taciturn's analysis downplays the stability and permanence of the ethical sphere, as if its limitations, which we are about to witness, render it inadequate in dealing with life's most pressing problems, for example the scandal of bad things happening to good people. From a contrary perspective, Sartre will proclaim and Camus will dramatize in his novel *The Plague*, that 'evil cannot be redeemed'. Such, at least, is the view of the atheistic existentialist. In any case, it is clear that what will later go by the name of 'existentialism' deals

4. Søren Kierkegaard, at the age of 41, a year before his death

Søren Kierkegaard (1813–55)

Known as the father of theistic existentialism, he was born in Copenhagen, where he lived all of his life. Schooled in theology and in Hegelian philosophy at the local university, he engaged in sharp polemics with the State Church, the popular press, and champions of Hegelian philosophy. Perhaps because he considered his personal calling a painful and lonely one, he broke his engagement with Regine Olsen, a member of a prominent local family, and remained celibate for the rest of his life. He published numerous philosophical and theological works, many under pseudonyms, distinguished by their sharp wit and psychological insights.

with specific individuals in concrete problematic situations. So let us follow these stages more closely.

The aesthetic stage

This is the sphere of the *immediate* temporally speaking. It has been observed that the range of differences it embraces could extend from plain philistinism to the greatest intellectual refinement. The person who lives at this stage, and one could do so for an entire lifetime, is focused on the present and remains indifferent to the past as repentance or the future as obligation except in a calculating manner geared to enhance the present, as we are about to see in the case of Johannes the Seducer. Kierkegaard was taken with the opera *Don Giovanni* – the tale of the unrepentant womanizer 'Don Juan' whose story as a tireless seducer of women was put to music by Mozart in one of the greatest operas ever written. The Don, whom Kierkegaard takes as a major model of the aesthetic sphere, lives only for the sensual satisfaction of the present moment. His presence haunts the descriptions in both *Stages* and *Either/Or*.

The first tale in *Stages* is the story of an ideal 'aesthetic' gathering entitled 'In Vino Veritas' (an ancient adage which might be translated as 'wine as truth serum'). It serves as the password for the occasion. The story is a parody of Plato's famous banquet of love, the *Symposium*. In both works, the emphasis is on drink and speeches in praise of love by the inebriated banqueters. But whereas Plato's party finally focuses on true, lasting *eros* that attends to the soul in contrast with the fleeting attraction of sensuous beauty, 'In Vino' is a celebration of sensuous beauty in its very fleetingness. In fact, the sheer immediacy and contingency of the event is underscored both by the delivery of the invitations at the last minute and the presence of the work crew ready to dismantle the gathering place immediately upon its conclusion. As one of the participants remarks: 'To be good, a thing must be all at once, for "at once" is the most divine of all categories . . . '. Recall Sartre's analysis of someone literally 'jumping for joy' in their vain attempt to condense a pleasant experience into a moment.

Tellingly, the revellers enter the banquet room to the strains of Mozart's opera. Their various speeches deal with erotic love or the quotidian relations between men and women. The concluding speech is given by one of Kierkegaard's characters, Johannes the Seducer, introduced in an earlier work, *Either/Or*. Since he personifies life in the aesthetic sphere, let us detail this domain by turning to his introduction in that prior volume.

'The Diary of a Seducer', one of Kierkegaard's most remarkable tales of life in the first sphere, recounts the machinations of 'Johannes the Seducer', whose tactics are a parody of the rakish progress of Don Juan. In fact, lines from the opera serve as an epigram at the start of the story. Johannes is attracted by a young woman of 16 years, Cordelia, whom he notices on the street in the company of her aunt who is also her guardian. He later encounters a young man, obviously smitten by the same girl, and proceeds to befriend him on the pretext of helping his suit. Having gained entrance to the girl's home as the young man's friend, Johannes proceeds to win the favour of the aunt even as he charms the maiden. The young man is soon dismissed from Johannes's company as now more of a liability than an asset. The story of the seduction and subsequent abandonment of the young Cordelia is recounted in a series of letters exchanged between them. Johannes seems quite indifferent to the pain he is causing, so intent is he on the 'ultimate enjoyment', after which he contrives to manoeuvre Cordelia into breaking their engagement so that she will assume responsibility for the separation. As Johannes remarks: 'The curse of an engagement is always on its ethical side. The ethical is just as tiresome in philosophy as in life. . . . I shall certainly manage it so that she will be the one who breaks the engagement.' No doubt, Johannes is less spontaneous than the Don. But his aim is the same: momentary conquest followed by abandonment without regret. Johannes captures the rich ambiguity of the term 'aesthetic' and of this existential sphere when he expostulates: 'To poetize oneself into a young girl is an art; to poetize oneself out of her is a masterpiece.' The aesthete is a kind of poet.

The ethical stage

Kierkegaard realizes that Johannes is not immoral; he simply fails to play the ethical game at all. The rules of right and wrong do not apply in his sphere of existence. Every consideration is aimed at the present, even if this 'present' lies in the future, as with the Seducer's calculations regarding Cordelia. There is no place here for the past as repentance or the future as obligation, defining features of the ethical sphere. The existentialist concept of 'commitment' is absent from this discourse. Repentance, obligation, and commitment are properly ethical categories and they come into play after a 'leap' or 'conversion' experience that is an exercise of free choice and thus an individuating act. In a move we shall elaborate shortly, this 'leap' is not the natural, much less, the necessary, evolution of the earlier stage, as a Hegelian reading of the situation would suggest. Kierkegaard seems to believe that most people live their entire lives in the aesthetic sphere. In any case, the aesthete, he argues, is incapable of the choice that enables him or her to be a self. As

Judge William, another of Kierkegaard's inventions, warns the young aesthete who, in *Either/Or*, has insisted that life is a masquerade:

> Do you not know that there comes a midnight hour when everyone has to throw off his mask? ... I have seen men in real life who so long deceived others that at last their true nature could not reveal itself. ... Or can you think of anything more frightful than that it might end with your nature being resolved into a multiplicity, that you really might become many, become, like those unhappy demoniacs, a legion and you thus would have lost the inmost and holiest thing of all in a man, the unifying power of personality? ... [Such a one] may be so inexplicably woven into relationships of life which extend far beyond himself, that he almost cannot reveal himself. But he who cannot reveal himself cannot love, and he who cannot love is the most unhappy man of all.

The Judge is articulating the general existentialist thesis that choice is self-constituting and liberating. Recall that, whereas Hegelian philosophy, in Kierkegaard's view, emphasizes 'mediation' between alternatives, which it raises to a higher, more comprehensive stage or standpoint, existential thinking stresses choice, the 'either/or' that involves risk, commitment, and individuation. With a particularly apt analogy, the Judge proposes:

> Think of the captain on his ship at the instant when it has to come about. He will perhaps be able to say 'I can either do this or that'; but in case he is not a pretty good navigator, he will be aware at the same time that the ship is all the while making its usual headway, and that therefore it is only an instant when it is indifferent whether he does this or that. So it is with a man. If he forgets to take account of the headway, there comes at last an instant when there no longer is any question of an either/or, not because he has chosen but because he has neglected to choose, which is equivalent to saying, because others have chosen for him, because he has lost his self.

This teaches the existentialist lesson that our entire life is an ongoing choice and that the failure to choose is itself a choice for which we are equally responsible. Sartre formulates this bluntly when he asserts that for human reality [the human being], to exist is to choose and to cease to choose is to cease to be. Sartre also echoes Kierkegaard's relation of choice to self-constitution when he adds that, for human reality, to be is to choose oneself.

The basic 'choice' that the Judge offers the young aesthete is what we have called a criterion-constituting choice. As he explains: 'My either/or does not in the first instance denote the choice between good and evil, it denotes the choice whereby one chooses good *and* evil/or excludes them.' In other words, it constitutes the decision to 'play the game' in which the categories of moral good and evil operate. In Kierkegaard's case, the defining feature of the moral is the universal and exceptionless nature of its rules. The ethic that Kierkegaard is proposing, derived from the work of the 18th-century German philosopher Immanuel Kant, takes the essence of the immoral to consist in holding yourself an exception to a rule that you want everyone else to observe. As Kant points out, the only reason we can lie or cheat or steal is that others will not do so. Its point is not simply that the social consequences of such a choice would be harmful, as the utilitarians (who hold that actions are right if they are of benefit to the majority) have argued, but that to universalize the practice, that is, to will that everyone do likewise, is a practical impossibility. For if everyone lied, nobody would be believed, thus rendering lying impossible. This also implies that such behaviour would reduce the others who obey moral rules to the status of mere instruments for the ends of the rule-breaker. This is a clear violation of the intrinsic value of each individual – a standard existentialist claim. We are dealing with a set of rules like the Ten Commandments or the Golden Rule, but formulated in non-religious terms. A person can be just or upright, as were Socrates and the Roman consul Brutus (who did not except his son from the death penalty for treason, though it lay in his power to do so), without being aware of Biblical directives. In fact, Socrates, by obeying the laws of Athens even when they condemned him unfairly, emerges as the model of the ethical sphere: he did not place himself above the general rule, though doing so caused him apparent harm. Kierkegaard designates these individuals 'tragic heroes' but adds that, unlike Abraham, 'the tragic hero still remains within the ethical'.

The religious stage

In Kierkegaard's view, the 'leap' of faith constitutes entrance into the religious sphere and the highest form of individuation. Here, the operative categories are neither pleasure and pain, as in the aesthetic sphere, nor good and evil, as in the ethical, but sin and grace. The model is Abraham, who in the story from Genesis was ready to sacrifice his only son in obedience to God's command, notwithstanding the Divine promise that the old man would be the father 'of many nations'. The temporal dimension of this extraordinary event is the 'instant' wherein this 'infinite' movement is made. The categories of the ethical are suspended in response to a divine command addressed to Abraham alone and by name. In this sense, the motives for the actions at the religious stage cannot be generalized as the ethical requires. In other words, the religious individual is 'beyond good and evil', in Nietzschean terms, and accordingly can be considered to be acting immorally. In ethical terms, Abraham has no words by which to explain his singular action to his wife. He can rely neither on the surety of general principles nor the support of universal reason. He is alone before God – the consummate individual. Abraham stands out from such anonymous refuge (he 'exists') in the most extreme manner. As he makes this move beyond the ethical, he experiences the anguish (*Angst*) of his freedom, even as he knows the risk that this command, so contrary to general moral principles, might not be Divine in origin. The religious individual is above the universal and, from that religious viewpoint, the 'temptation' now is to reverse this relationship, namely to make the ethical/universal absolute, to do the 'moral' thing and disobey the Divine command. This is truly a 'leap' of faith.

It has been argued that Kierkegaard's interpretation of this Biblical story unwittingly gave rise to what is known as 'situation ethics' associated with Nietzschean and Sartrean existentialism. This is an approach to moral decision-making that considers each ethical case to be unique and incomparable, except in a general rule-of-thumb manner. Thus Sartre speaks of a young man faced with the choice of staying in Nazi-occupied France with his mother, whose husband was suspected of collaboration and whose first son had been killed in the German offensive of 1940, or of leaving the country to fight with the Free French forces. Were he to seek advice from a party considered favourable to one or the other decision, he would in effect already have made his choice. Instead, Sartre dares: 'You are free, therefore choose – that is to say, invent.' As he explains: 'No rule of general morality can show you what you ought to do; no signs are vouchsafed in this world. The Catholics will reply, "Oh, but there are!" Very well; still, it is I myself, in every case, who have to interpret the signs.' The perils and the fruits of 'moral creativity' are an underlying theme in existentialist writing, especially as exhibited by Nietzsche, Sartre, and de Beauvoir.

Certainly, Kierkegaard did not propose that one reject the ethical. Indeed, he referred to Abraham's act as the 'teleological *suspension* of the ethical', not to its abandonment. The ethical sphere was being placed on hold for a higher goal, or *telos*, namely fidelity to the Divine command. As Abraham descends the mountain where the sacrifice of Isaac was to have taken place (an angel had stayed his hand, indicating that Abraham had passed the test of unconditional faith in God), he is returning to the ethical sphere but with a difference. He now knows that it is not exceptionless and that his observance of its precepts and rules are based on a higher loyalty. In the final analysis, as Kierkegaard summarizes, the individual is above the universal. Standard moral rules are no longer absolute in the sense of demanding to be followed by all and always.

This raises the issue of the relation among these spheres and the unity of a life. Speaking of the 'dissipation' of life in the aesthetic

5. Abraham about to sacrifice his son Isaac

sphere, namely its fragmentation and squandering, the Judge warns
the young aesthete: '[In your present state] you are incapable of
love because love means self-giving and you have no self to give.'
And he refers to the interrelation of the spheres as if the meaning of
life depended on the integration of all three: 'If you cannot reach the
point of seeing the aesthetical, the ethical, and the religious as three
great allies, if you do not know how to conserve the unity of the
diverse appearances which everything assumes in these diverse
spheres, then life is devoid of meaning, then one must grant that
you are justified in maintaining your pet theory that one can say
of everything, "Do it or don't do it – you will regret both".' The
alternative to such a synthesis, in the case of this aesthete, at least,
seems to be scepticism and/or nihilism.

Kierkegaard is not entirely consistent in his account of these stages
or spheres. On the one hand, he stresses the 'either/or' that
catapults one from one state to the other. Individuating choice is

clearly at the core of each move. And there seems to be no simple
return to the prior sphere after the leap has occurred. Once having
chosen to play the ethical game, as it were, one cannot reconsider
and return to the purely aesthetic without qualification. You have
lost your innocence, literally, and now can resume your hedonistic
behaviour only as an immoral person. By parity of reasoning, it
would seem, the lonely individual who had made the leap of
religious faith cannot backslide to the merely aesthetic or even to
the purely ethical (as if the experience of its limits had not occurred)
without incurring the penalty of 'sin' – a properly religious category,
though Kierkegaard sometimes conflates it with ethical vice. And
yet, as we have just observed, the point of seeing these spheres as
'three great allies' implies either a Hegelian 'synthesis' (return of the
repressed) or an 'overlap' that resonates more fully with the image
of sphere than with that of stage. In either case, the guiding theme
of individuating 'choice' is seriously compromised. Admittedly, one
of the advantages of such indirect communication as Kierkegaard's
use of pseudonyms (or Nietzsche's of allegories, or even Plato's of
dialogues) is that one does not have to seek consistency among the
voices. As we shall see, the existentialists prize ambiguity. But, to
repeat, they are not irrationalists. They aim to make sense insofar as
sense can be made in and out of our contingent world.

Freedom but not for all: Nietzsche

Existentialism is a philosophy of freedom, even if these thinkers do
not agree on the precise meaning of that basic term. Nietzsche, for
one, famously denied the notion of free will and the moral choice
that it exercises. His project of bringing the human being back to
earth and away from its illusions about the transcendent and
eternal turned him toward the biological dimension of human
existence, its irrational instincts and drives: what he called
'will-to-power', which, despite its popular association with choice
and dominance, is really the answer to the metaphysical question
'What is there, ultimately?' – and this, notwithstanding his animus
against metaphysics. Taken in its cosmic sense, will-to-power is the

force that moves the universe; understood biologically, it is the irresistible life impetus that drives the biosphere; psychologically, it is the drive to dominate and control. Its 'highest' expression is the self-control exercised by the free spirits for whom Nietzsche reserves a 'higher' morality than the chiefly religious ethics of the herd. As French philosopher Michel Haar observes, 'Nature as a whole is will-to-power', and it manifests itself in every dimension of existence. This is why philosopher Paul Ricoeur could list Nietzsche among the 'masters of suspicion', along with Marx and Freud. Each thinker casts doubt on our ostensive accounts of why we do what we do. The real reason for our behaviour, they claim, lay elsewhere. In Nietzsche's case, that ultimate source is will-to-power. As Foucault will later say in a Nietzschean mode, the most high-minded efforts at penal reform in the early 19th century, for example, were ultimately expressions of the desire for more effective control of populations.

What place is there, then, in such a universe for creative freedom in the existentialist sense? What is the ground for the responsibility that we feel in ourselves and ascribe to others? This is the perennial problem of freedom versus determinism, but given a more dramatic twist as befits an existentialist version. In a universe where every event has a cause and every cause is necessitating (both claims open to dispute), no place seems left for the 'absolute beginnings' that popular understanding of existentialist freedom proclaims. Every event has an antecedent (whether natural or cultural according to the kind of determinism one is proposing) and every cause is necessitating. In effect, under this description, nobody could have acted otherwise than they did.

The 'error' of free will, Nietzsche insists, is the belief that choice rather than physiological and cultural forces is the basis of our judgements of moral approval and disapproval. Displaying his predilection for psychological rather than ontological explanations, he remarks: 'The evil acts at which we are most indignant rest on the error that he who perpetrates them against us possesses free

6. Nietzsche's intense gaze

Friedrich Nietzsche (1844–1900)

Born in Röcken, Germany. Such was his recognized brilliance that he was named professor of philology at the University of Basel before he had received his doctorate. Burdened with poor health most of his life, he resigned his professorship after ten years and spent the next decade moving around Europe, writing essays known for their caustic wit and affirmation of life. The father of 'atheistic' existentialism, his most famous pronouncement is 'God is dead', meaning that modern science has rendered belief in the Divine irrelevant. His self-appointed task was to combat the nihilism that this event entailed. He succumbed to insanity during the last decade of his life.

will, that is to say, that he could have *chosen* not to cause us this harm.' If Nietzsche is correct, it would seem to follow that our tolerance could know no bounds because, to quote the pre-Romantic French novelist Madame de Staël, 'to understand all is to forgive all'. Though this may be the wisdom of Spinoza and his German admirer, it is scarcely the common sense of the herd.

But Nietzsche, in his allegory of a religious prophet, *Zarathustra*, sets forth the possibility of a 'higher' ethic based on the freedom/ ability to create values. In a sense, with the 'death of God', that is, with the increasing irrelevance of the idea of the Judaeo-Christian God, the 'free' spirits (Nietzsche's true individuals) are challenged to assume divine prerogatives, among which the most important is that of creating life-affirming moral and life-enhancing aesthetic values. 'Man is an evaluating animal', Nietzsche claims, and moral values of nobility and aesthetic values of the beautiful coalesce in the project of making of one's life a work of art. This union of the noble and the beautiful can save us from ourselves as it did the Ancient Greeks; that is, from the despair arising out of our realization that the Universe does not care. Art is to supplant religion for Nietzsche, just as it would later promise a kind of salvation to Anton Roquentin, the protagonist in Sartre's philosophical novel *Nausea*. So it seems that an ethics of freedom is available to those 'free spirits' who have the ears to hear and the courage to affirm what they hear. Could they have done otherwise, those free spirits? Nietzsche seems to dismiss this as a false problem raised by the erroneous belief in free will. In fact, they will not do 'otherwise', if they are truly free spirits, since it follows from their nobility of birth or character to act in just this manner.

Nietzsche sees our current Judaeo-Christian ethics as the result of an exercise of will-to-power on the part of 'slaves' who reversed, or 'transvalued', an original 'master' morality. In Nietzsche's fabulous account, the original 'pagan' leaders subscribed to a life-affirming morality of the noble and the ignoble. These values were the very opposite of what we know as Judaeo-Christian morality. Motivated by *ressentiment* against the masters' life-affirming and unvarnished exercise of will-to-power, Nietzsche hypothesizes, the priestly class of the slaves inverted the master's values into their own categories of what today we call moral 'good and evil' by a covert exercise of will-to-power. Thus the masters' good and bad (noble and ignoble) was transvalued into the slaves' evil and good respectively. What the masters had considered good, the slaves condemned as evil and what they disdained as ignoble became the slaves' 'virtues' of humility, pity, and the like. Nietzsche preaches a higher morality to the 'free spirits' which consists of a reversal of the slaves' transvaluation such that selfishness is converted from a slavish vice to a masterly virtue and so forth. This new (or older) morality is thus 'beyond good and evil' of Judaeo-Christian ethics but subscribes to the 'good and bad' of the master morality. Where the master's exercise of will-to-power was relatively open and unbridled, that of the slaves was marked by a covert, life-denying *ressentiment*. The reversal that Nietzsche teaches the free spirits is essentially life-affirming once more. But it is only for the few.

Nietzsche proposes to those who can bear it a doctrine of fatalism that is even more challenging to the existentialist spirit than the determinism just discussed. According to this theory, we are fated to do just what we do. Nietzsche calls this the thesis of 'eternal recurrence'. He thinks it follows from the fact that our options are finite but time is infinite. Thus, as he interprets it, whatever can happen will occur again an infinite number of times. If determinism is retrospective, fatalism is prospective; it concerns what is written in the book of life, the pages of which have yet to be turned. Given this situation, Nietzsche's recommendation is not passive resignation but active 'love of fate' (*amor fati*) as the ancient Stoics preached. We shall review Camus's version of this doctrine later on. But whether one takes this theory literally or, more plausibly, reads it as a moral imperative to act with courage and circumspection, 'redeeming the past by a resolute act of will', as Zarathustra urges, it raises the issue again of how 'free' we are to follow or to reject Nietzsche's counsel. And this is a paradox worthy of Kierkegaard.

Curiously, Kierkegaard's Judge William faces his hapless young aesthete with a somewhat analogous challenge by referring to a kind of psycho-social conditioning:

> For me the instant of choice is very serious . . . because . . . [of the] danger that the next instant it may not be equally in my power to choose, that something already has lived which must be lived over again. To think that for an instant one can keep one's personality a blank, or that strictly speaking one can break off and bring to a halt the course of the personal life is a delusion. The personality is already interested in the choice before one chooses, and when the choice is postponed the personality chooses unconsciously, or the choice is made by obscure powers within it. So when at last the choice is made, one discovers (unless, as I remarked before, the

personality has been completely volatilized) that there is something which must be done over again, something which must be revoked, and this is often very difficult.

In the case of Kierkegaard, the choice is reciprocal with the 'self' that it both constitutes and expresses. 'Personality' here resembles more Nietzsche's underlying 'instinct' that urges the decision and serves as its default mode. Or, perhaps better, it functions like a habit that is the sedimentation of previous choices, in which case the autonomy of existential choice can be preserved.

Sartre wrote an essay entitled 'Cartesian Freedom' where he developed the Nietzschean view that, in the absence of belief in God, we should assume the absolute freedom that Descartes had ascribed to the Divinity. In phenomenological terms, this meant that the entire 'world' (the horizon of our meanings) is our creation for which we hold total responsibility. 'We are without excuse', he insisted. Like Nietzsche, Sartre focused chiefly on the creation of moral values, as we have seen. But unlike his predecessor, he claimed that these values were the result of our creative 'choices'. Nietzsche, on the contrary, seems to believe that 'those who can hear', that is, the free spirits, are genetically capable of being moved by the force of his arguments, which elude or threaten the herd. If so, he is subscribing to a kind of psycho-biological determinism (we must follow what we perceive to be the strongest argument and only the free spirits are capable of appreciating those motives that are properly life-affirming). This certainly separates him from Sartre and de Beauvoir but not unambiguously from Kierkegaard, as we have just seen.

'To philosophize in view of the exception'

The first one to propound a philosophy of *Existenz* was the German psychiatrist and philosopher Karl Jaspers. Though he devoted many pages to Nietzsche and very few to Kierkegaard, it was probably the latter who influenced him more. Jaspers was the first major thinker to discuss them as a pair. Despite their contradictory views on the existence of God, Jaspers considered Kierkegaard and Nietzsche to be the major thinkers of the 19th century after Hegel and the ones whose works most effectively set the stage for 20th-century European thought. As the Nazi regime was strengthening its grip on German society and culture in 1935, Jaspers, a courageously anti-Nazi figure, spoke the following in a public lecture: 'Regarding the situation of philosophizing as well as of real life, Kierkegaard and Nietzsche articulate the impending calamity which at that time no one had become aware of (except as momentary, quickly forgotten presentiments) but which became clear to them.' That calamity was the devaluing of what Jaspers called *Existenz* (the properly human way of existing) for the sake of a naive form of scientific knowledge. Without slipping into irrationalism and with due respect for the power as well as the limits of reason to guide our lives, both Kierkegaard and Nietzsche criticized 'systematic' accounts such as Hegel offered of our elusive and ambiguous existence. Each spoke to the individual, the one who had the spirit to be able to understand and accept what they were teaching. It was in this regard that Kierkegaard cited the 18th-century German scientist and satirist Georg Christoph Lichtenberg's epigram: 'Such works are mirrors; if a monkey peeks in, no apostle can peek out.'

In Jaspers's eyes, both men pursued the values of honesty, commitment, and 'authentic truth' beyond the limit of their physical and psychological endurance. They were truly exceptions, to be admired but not imitated. No one is obliged to martyrdom, he seemed to be saying. Like Socrates, they lived and suffered the authenticity of their teaching. Their lives were what Jaspers called 'shipwreck'. As such, they stand as warnings of the excess that we should not follow but likewise as models of the virtues we should emulate. This inspires Jaspers's lesson from their lives: 'To philosophize in view of the exception without being an exception'.

Chapter 3
Humanism: for and against

Heroism and sanctity don't really appeal to me, I imagine.
What interests me is being a man.

Albert Camus, *The Plague*

If there is a humanism today, it rids itself of the illusion Valéry
designated so well in speaking of 'that little man within man whom
we always presuppose.'

Maurice Merleau-Ponty

On 29 October 1945, Sartre delivered a public lecture entitled 'Is
Existentialism a Humanism?' that was soon to become the manifesto
of the existentialist movement. From all accounts, it was truly an
intellectual event. It certainly fuelled the flames of the movement
that was spreading from the Left-Bank cafes and music halls of Paris
to similar haunts across Europe and around the world. Delivered to
an overflow crowd, it summarized briefly what came to be known as
the defining characteristic of Sartrean existentialism: the claim that
'existence precedes essence'. Given the postulated atheism of Sartre's
view, it seemed to follow that individuals were left to create their own
values because there was no moral order in the universe by which
they could guide their actions, indeed, that this freedom was itself the
ultimate value to which one could appeal (as he put it, 'in choosing
anything at all, I first of all choose freedom'). Now this much could
have been gleaned by anyone who had read his masterwork,

Being and Nothingness, published two years earlier. But that long and difficult book was not exactly a bestseller and, one could add, like Darwin's *The Origin of Species*, it was more often cited than read.

What made this lecture necessary was not only that it rendered more accessible many of the basic claims of the larger work, but that it attempted to answer the objections of Sartre's leading critics from both the Communists and the Catholics that this new philosophy was the incarnation of bourgeois individualism and that it was totally insensitive to the demands of social justice felt by war-ravaged European society. In other words, the leading voice of existentialist thought was challenged to answer the claims that his was just another narcissistic opiate to divert the youth from the task of rebuilding a just society out of the ruins of the Fascist tragedy. Existentialism would lose its credibility to the larger public if it could not present a viable and relevant social philosophy.

Such a task could scarcely be met in an evening's lecture. Indeed, the strength and weakness of this brief talk lay in its attempt to do so. Sartre appealed to Kant's ethic of universal principles (the ones that Kierkegaard's Abraham had suspended for a higher goal) when he said that no one could be free in a concrete sense (and not merely in the abstract sense employed in *Being and Nothingness* that defines the individual as free) unless everyone were free. 'In choosing, I choose for all people', he insisted. And in words that carry a distinctively Kantian ring, Sartre challenges that each agent ought to say to himself: 'Am I he who has the right to act such that humanity regulates itself by my acts?' This seemed to convey a sense of responsibility for the other person and even for society as a whole that was different from his previous contentions. Sartre introduced yet another ethical principle when he asserted that in every moral choice we form an image of the kind of person we want to be and, indeed, of what any moral person should be: 'For in effect, there is not one of our acts that, in creating the man we wish to be, does not at the same time create an *image* of man such as we judge he *ought* to be.' However relevant these principles might be for constructing a social ethic, neither seemed to follow from what Sartre had published thus far. In light of his subsequent work on a social ontology (see Chapter 5), these remarks are prescient. But they enter this lecture like a foreign body to save the individualist from his Marxist and religious critics. What we are witnessing, in effect, is Sartre thinking aloud, and philosophizing 'on the wing'. The inconsistencies of this lecture, while of interest for charting the evolution of his thought, were obviously an embarrassment to him. In fact, this is the only piece that he ever openly regretted having published. Ironically, it seems to be his one philosophical work that everyone reads.

In arguing that existentialism is a humanistic philosophy, Sartre means that it places the human being at the centre of its attention and at the apex of its value-hierarchy. Though he mentions theistic existentialists in this lecture, citing Jaspers and Marcel as examples, it is difficult to find room for them in the body of his speech. Rather, he insists that the ultimate value, the goal of our endeavours, should be the fostering of the freedom of the individual, by which he means the enhancement of his or her concrete possibilities of choice. That creative freedom, he implies, should not be sacrificed to any 'higher' value, whether it be the 'class' of the Marxists or the 'God' of the religious believers. This echoes the image of what Nietzsche called 'free spirits' in his *Human, All Too Human*. When Sartre insists that one must 'choose, that is invent', he doesn't mean simply 'improvise'. Rather, he is referring to the responsible decision to opt for or against freedom itself.

Agreeing with Sartre and Nietzsche that whatever meaning our world may harbour is created by individuals either alone or in social relations, Albert Camus views this as the source of our anguish: we long for meaning conveyed by a Universe that cares but discover only an empty sky. What are we to do in the face of what he calls the 'absurdity' of this situation? Camus offers existential solace in his interpretation of the Greek myth of Sisyphus, the mortal condemned by the gods to push a stone up a mountain only to see it roll back down repeatedly for all eternity. And yet Camus claims to consider Sisyphus happy at the moment he turns to retrieve the rock once more at the base of the hill. Why happy? Because Sisyphus has risen above his fate, not by dull resignation but by *deliberate choice*. He thereby shows himself superior to this inanimate rock. In Nietzsche's words, he has turned the 'it was' (his past, the givens of his situation) into the 'thus I willed it'.

Faced with this parable of the ultimate futility of life, Camus counsels that our only hope is to acknowledge that there is no ultimate hope. Like the Ancient Stoics, we must limit our expectations in view of our mortality.

7. **The only hope is to know there is no (ultimate) hope**

Humanism and the unconscious

The mantra of Sartrean humanism, echoed by Camus and de Beauvoir, is that you can always make something out of what you've been made into. So the almost proverbial existentialist 'pessimism' harbours a deep, if limited, hope. This was the message of Camus's 'The Myth of Sisyphus', as it was of Nietzsche's embrace of fate (*amor fati*). It is the major humanistic consequence of Sartre's rejection of the Freudian unconscious, namely that such drives and forces rob us of our freedom and responsibility.

Not all existentialists are so suspicious of the unconscious as such. We have witnessed Kierkegaard's Judge William refer to unconscious choices and obscure powers. In view of Nietzsche's claims regarding non-rational instincts and drives, one can appreciate Freud's admission that Nietzsche anticipated him in several respects. And if Heidegger was said to be indifferent to psychoanalysis, he nonetheless addressed a group of its practitioners on several occasions at the request of his close friend, the Swiss psychoanalyst Menard Boss. In fact, Ludwig Binswanger fashioned an influential approach to psychoanalysis that relied on Heideggerian concepts. Merleau-Ponty's attitude towards the unconscious seemed to be ambiguous. Indeed, he thought the unconscious was not a fully developed idea for Freud himself. He believed that Freud's term approximated to what other thinkers more appropriately named 'ambiguous perception' or 'non-reflective perception', a view that Sartre would have shared. In any case, Merleau-Ponty respected Freudian psychoanalysis throughout his career. Even Sartre's famous opposition is subject to question. As his former pupil and distinguished psychoanalyst Jean-Bertrand Pontalis observed, some day the history of Sartre's 30-year-long relationship with psychoanalysis, an ambiguous mixture of equally deep attraction and repulsion, will have to be written and perhaps his work reinterpreted in light of it. Karl Jaspers, a psychiatrist whose major study, *General Psychopathology*, Sartre helped translate into French in the 1920s, speaks of the 'inaccessible ground of human awareness'.

But the Freudian unconscious attracts their ire. That same Jaspers, sounding like Sartre, is critical of the Freudian view that 'man is the puppet of his unconscious, and [that] when the latter has had a clear light thrown upon it, he will become master of himself'. In contrast, Jaspers objects that:

> the self-examination of a sincere thinker, which after the long-lasting Christian interlude attained its climax in Kierkegaard and Nietzsche, is in psychoanalysis degraded into the discovery of sexual longings and typical experiences of childhood; it is the masking of genuine but hazardous self-examination by the mere rediscovery of familiar types in a realm of reputed necessity wherein the lower levels of human life are regarded as having an absolute validity.

Among this group, then, only Merleau-Ponty showed a strong interest in the Freudian unconscious as well as in its French, structuralist version promoted by psychoanalyst Jacques Lacan (1901–81). And lest one conclude that acceptance of the Freudian unconscious is incompatible with existential humanism overall, one should note the Nietzschean possibility of 'self-mastery' that psychoanalysis sought to fulfil and which Jaspers questions. What is at issue is the kind of freedom that one can expect of an embodied and socially situated agent. Existentialists seem divided on this matter.

An alternative (to) humanism?

I have not yet discussed the thought of Martin Heidegger at any length. It is even argued by many of his followers that this major European philosopher was not an existentialist at all. It certainly must be conceded that Heidegger's stated interest was in the question of the meaning of Being and not in the ethical or psychological issues that concerned Kierkegaard and Sartre. He asked in his major work, *Being and Time* (1927), 'What does it mean to be?' And his later writings evince a rather poetic, not to say mystical, concentration on removing the obstacles in our cultural and personal lives to the occurrence of what he called the Being-event. In other words, throughout his career, Heidegger was critical of those who distracted our attention from gaining access to Being by concentrating on metaphysical questions of essence and existence, cause and effect, subject and object, and theories of human nature.

In his famous *Letter on Humanism* (1947), written ostensibly in response to Sartre's lecture just mentioned, Heidegger is critical of traditional humanism with its definition of 'man' as a 'rational animal' or an 'animal endowed with speech'. Such a conception, in Heidegger's view, sells man short and easily leads to the kind of technological society that defines man in terms of productivity and assesses all values in terms of personal or social utility. Heidegger sees Sartre as failing to escape this traditional

Martin Heidegger (1889–1976)

Raised in the mountains of southwest Germany, Heidegger never lost his love of nature or his respect for the simple life. Educated at the University of Freiburg im Breisgau, where he served as assistant to Edmund Husserl, his first book, *Being and Time* (1927), was recognized by his colleagues as a work of genius. It introduced a hermeneutical phenomenology that differed from that of more orthodox Husserlians. Still, on Husserl's recommendation, he succeeded him in the chair of philosophy at Freiburg. His subsequent involvement with the National Socialist (Nazi) Party remains the topic of much dispute. But his reputation as a major philosopher is secure.

8. Heidegger, the garden, and the forest beyond

metaphysics and the philosophical anthropology that it
engenders. The glory of 'man' (or what Heidegger calls *Dasein*,
meaning the human way of being) is his openness to Being. It is
his ability to conserve a place in the world for what Heidegger
calls the occurrence of Being. In a well-known expression from
his later work, Heidegger calls man/*Dasein* 'the shepherd of

Being'. It is his glory to remain open and attentive to the 'call' or the dimension of the 'holy' that eludes our daily concerns. Heidegger counsels that we should learn to 'dwell poetically' rather than behaving merely pragmatically. If one accepts this advice, then the later Heidegger can be seen as preaching the 'true' humanism, one that underscores the most profound possibilities of the human. That was his claim in this *Letter*.

But we should add that such discourse seems far distant from the existentialist themes and theses we have been discussing thus far. In fact, the earlier Heidegger, the author of *Being and Time*, adopts many Kierkegaardian and Nietzschean concepts to elucidate how we gain access to a Being of which we already have some inkling. He employs a 'hermeneutical', or interpretive, method to articulate that basic inkling. The unpacking of that pre-understanding brings his existentialist relevance to the fore. Though we shall pursue the matter at greater length in our final chapter, we should note here that such concepts as *Angst* (existential anguish) and ekstatic temporality, already discussed, figure centrally in his early thought. So too does the notion of our mortal temporality (our being-unto-death), the realization and positive acceptance of which serve both to concretize our finitude and to open us to the meaning of Being by facing us with the possibility of our ceasing to be.

The novelist Saul Bellow captures this Heideggerian insight with the rumination of the character Moses Herzog in his book of that title:

> But what is the philosophy of this generation? Not God is dead, that point was passed long ago. Perhaps it should be stated Death is God. This generation thinks – and this is its thought of thoughts – that nothing faithful, vulnerable, fragile can be durable or have any true power. Death waits for these things as a cement floor waits for a dropping light bulb. The brittle shell of glass loses its tiny vacuum

with a burst, and that is that. And this is how we teach metaphysics on each other.

But it would be ontology (the approach to Being) rather than metaphysics (the study of the ultimate categories by which to order our thoughts) that would interest Heidegger here. The unifying power of our personal mortality to gather the dissipation of our busyness and distraction in average everyday concerns carries a 'humanistic' significance that Sartre could recognize, even if Heidegger would claim that, by concentrating on the moral and psychological aspects of our mortality rather than on its power to reveal what it means to be, the existentialist is failing to see the forest for the trees.

In the final analysis, however one may describe Heidegger's overall philosophical project, one can scarcely deny that he contributed significantly to the movement and that his early works can fruitfully sustain an 'existentialist' reading.

Creative freedom versus creative fidelity: theistic humanism

We saw Sartre give brief mention to theistic existentialists in his lecture and then proceed to discuss existentialism in terms that seem to exclude or at least to discount belief in God. But not all humanism is atheistic. In fact, in a manner analogous to that of Heidegger, theists argue that atheism degrades the true worth of the human being by reducing him or her to a mere product of nature, without intrinsic value or ultimate hope. Again, much turns on the kind of freedom or autonomy that the would-be existentialist accords the individual. Atheists claim that such freedom is absolute. Whatever perfections humans have ascribed to God, they insist, have been gained at their own expense and theology is simply anthropology upside down. Nietzsche's thesis about the death of God leads him to advocate a heroic atheism by which one forges ahead like Sisyphus despite the presumed indifference of the Universe.

Theists, on the contrary, argue that the distinguishing feature of the human being is his or her openness, not just to Heideggerian Being (though some would interpret Heidegger in a vaguely theistic manner), but to a Deity that understands and cares. For them, freedom is genuine but created. They view the world and our existence as a gift and an invitation to a loving response. Our resultant attitude should be one of what Gabriel Marcel calls 'creative fidelity' to this gift. Like Heidegger, Marcel rejects the idolatry of the technical world and the calculative thinking that fosters it. (Heidegger had argued that the triumph of the technical in contemporary society and the reduction of both nature and

9. Marcel, the philosopher of hope, looking avuncular

Gabriel Marcel (1889–1973)

A Parisian all his life, he was the first to apply the term 'existentialist' to Sartre. In reaction to the dominant idealist philosophy of his day, he wished to be a philosopher of the concrete. With the exception of the prestigious Gifford Lectures, published as *The Mystery of Being* (1950), most of his philosophical writings, starting with his *Metaphysical Journal* (1927), were in the mode of meditations. A convert to Catholicism, he maintained a strongly religious dimension. Exhibiting the existentialist union of philosophy and imaginative literature, he suggested that his philosophical thought might best be discovered in his more than 30 published plays.

humans to mere 'resources' were the logical outcome of our forgetfulness of Being over the centuries and our desire to control, culminating in Nietzsche's doctrine of the will-to-power.) In stark contrast with Camus's rejection of any ultimate hope, Marcel's focus is precisely on the nuances of human hope, which is tied to faithfulness and confidence in an Other's promise but not to the calculable guarantee of some impersonal force. As if explicitly to counter Camus's position, Marcel insists that metaphysically speaking, the only genuine hope is hope in what does not depend on ourselves, hope springing from humility and not from pride.

Karl Jaspers elaborates a concept of 'philosophical faith' that he distinguishes both from the faith of revealed religion and from atheism. Such faith entails an attitude towards 'Transcendence' as the deepest potentiality of our own *Existenz* and it articulates our experience of our own finitude in such 'limit situations' as suffering, guilt, and death. Broadly analogous to Heidegger's

10. Karl Jaspers and his world

Karl Jaspers (1883–1969)

Born into a wealthy family in Oldenburg, Germany, and trained in medicine, his first major publication was *General Psychopathology* (1913). He soon shifted to philosophy, publishing *Psychologie der Weltanschauungen* (1919) and receiving the chair of philosophy at Heidelberg in 1921. He was the first to call his approach '*Existenz* philosophy'. A theistic existentialism, it focused on such 'limit situations' as suffering, guilt, and death. To experience these is to sense both our finitude and intimations of what he calls 'Transcendence', or the ground of our *Existenz*. For 'political unreliability', the Nazis removed him from his professorship in 1937.

being-unto-death, Jaspers's concept of death as a limit situation, for example, brings to our attention a dimension of *Existenz* that eludes our conceptualization. In this manner, we gain access to Transcendence indirectly and not by means of standard rational argument. For Jaspers, Transcendence is the absolute Other that grounds our *Existenz*. Like Marcel, he speaks of *Existenz* as the gift of this non-objectifiable Being that he calls Transcendence, and like Heidegger, he insists that Transcendence shows itself only to *Existenz* (which functions like Heidegger's *Dasein*, namely denoting the human way of being). Only humans ponder why they exist at all. And this raises the characteristically existentialist issue of our contingent existence.

The experience of contingency

The work that made Sartre's early reputation was his philosophical novel *Nausea*. In an oft-cited passage, his character Anton Roquentin is seated on a park bench contemplating the root of a chestnut tree:

> It took my breath away. Never before these last few days, had I understood what 'to exist' meant. . . . There we were, the whole lot of us, awkward, embarrassed by our own existence, having no reason to be here rather than there; confused, vaguely restless, feeling superfluous to one another. Superfluity was the only relationship I could establish between these trees, these hedges, these paths. Vainly I strove to compute the number of the chestnut trees, or their distance from the Velleda, or their height as compared with that of the plane trees; each of them escaped from the pattern I made for it, overflowed from it or withdrew. And I too among them, vile, languorous, obscene, chewing the cud of my thoughts, I too was superfluous. [I is you or I or anyone.] Luckily I did not feel it, I only understood it, but I felt uncomfortable because I was afraid of feeling it. . . . I thought vaguely of doing away with myself, to do away with at least one of these superfluous existences. But my death – my corpse, my blood poured out on this gravel, among these

plants, in this smiling garden – would have been superfluous as well. I was superfluous to all eternity.

In several respects this imaginative description, like Saul Bellow's 'falling light bulb', constitutes an existentialist 'argument'. It also exhibits the close relation that obtains between existentialist philosophy and imaginative literature. Not that it proves or even explains but that it enables us vicariously to experience and so, as Husserl said, to see; that is, it articulates an experience with which we resonate: 'Yes, that's how it is.' In the present case, the experience is of our own contingency, of the sheer fact that we are and that we do not have to be. It's not simply the obvious fact that, had our parents never met, 'we' would not be here. Rather, existentialists of all stripes appeal to that philosophically recurrent insight which fixes on the distinction between 'what' we are and 'that' we are at all, underscoring our experience of *non*-necessity. What are we to make of this?

It is the humanist dimension of existentialism that comes to grips with the fact of our sheer being there. And it is their respective responses to the questions 'Why do we exist?', 'Why is there anything at all rather than nothing?', that distinguish the theists from the atheists among them. Unlike philosophers such as Bertrand Russell who deny that the question is even meaningful, the existentialists, both theistic and atheist, take it quite seriously. And how they respond colours the 'humanism' they propose. We saw that, for Camus, we were challenged to make the most of an absurd situation. Sartre would agree with Roquentin that our existence is just a brute fact, that we are superfluous (*de trop*). And both would subscribe to the Sisyphean concluding line of Sartre's play *No Exit*, 'Well, let's get on with it.' Just because there is not ultimate hope does not mean that we are bereft of all hope whatsoever. The wisdom of Sisyphus is not to make the rock stay put but to get the thing off his toe! We are advised to pursue limited but attainable goods – like the Ancient Stoics.

Does hope for something beyond our own efforts discredit our fundamental worth or limit our possibilities? The theists attend to the seemingly natural drive to transcend our limits in hope and aspiration. Speaking of this passage from Sartre's novel, Marcel remarks:

> I shall take it for granted that this experience is genuine; an account of it must form the preamble to any analysis of Sartre's anthropology, and I should like to say at once that, taken in itself, it appears to me irrefutable. Our problem – and it is a difficult problem – is to know what value to assign to it.

Is our existence a brute fact to be dealt with or a gift to be accepted in a spirit of thankfulness? Suggesting his own alternative, Marcel remarks that the materiality of the tree root and of his own existence 'is experienced by Sartre not as overabundance of being but as fundamental and absurd'. Marcel, on the contrary, would experience it as a marvellous superabundance of being and an arresting instance of the ancient Platonic principle that the good tends to diffuse itself like a love that insists on being communicated or an experience of beauty that demands to be shared.

Humanisms and freedoms (Merleau-Ponty)

In the midst of the controversy generated by Sartre's seminal lecture, his friend and fellow philosopher, Maurice Merleau-Ponty, published an essay, 'The Battle Over Existentialism', that framed the controversy in terms of humanism. The question, he observed, 'is to know what part freedom plays and whether we can allow it something without giving it everything'. That sober remark summarized the issue neatly: what is the proper place of the human being in the material and cultural world? Against the materialists, specifically the Marxist dialectical materialists, existentialism argues that the human being is more than the sum of physical, psychological, and social forces. That 'more' is our consciousness, by which we can assess and respond to these very forces. But against the 'spiritualists', and he had in mind the religious Right, as we would say today, the existentialist emphasizes our situatedness, beginning with our embodiedness that gives us a perspective and frustrates every attempt to volatilize our existence into that of some free-floating spirit hovering over the world. As Merleau-Ponty insisted (and Marcel agreed), I do not have a body, I *am* my body. It is between these extremes that the existentialist tries to make sense of his or her existence. Merleau-Ponty explains:

> The merit of this new philosophy is precisely that it tries, in the notion of existence, to find a way of thinking about our condition. In the modern sense of the word, 'existence' is that movement through which man is in the world and involves himself in a physical and social situation which then becomes his point of view on the world.

Classical philosophy, such as that of Descartes, related us to the world primarily through knowledge. We saw how existentialists rejected what they took to be Husserl's continuance of this Cartesian prejudice in his phenomenological method. Existentialism claims that we are in the world by a relationship of being in which, paradoxically, the subject *is* our body, our world, and our situation, by a sort of exchange. As Heidegger said, *Dasein* is in the world initially through its practical concerns and not its theoretical cognition. Merleau-Ponty explains this by focusing his attention on the primacy of our lived bodies.

Though Merleau-Ponty will move beyond existentialism towards the end of his life, cut short by sudden death at the age of 53, his contribution to existentialist thought was chiefly in his close analysis of our bodily being and of the 'interworld' of social existence that the early Sartre seemed to discount, if not ignore completely. Merleau-Ponty's early work in experimental psychology distinguished him from most existentialists, who, except for Jaspers, seemed rather indifferent to empirical science. And, as we shall see in Chapter 6, inspired by the newly emerging structural linguistics, he gradually came to make language the focal point of his reflections, enriching, if not displacing, his vintage phenomenological descriptions.

Chapter 4
Authenticity

The choice of authenticity appears to be a *moral* decision.

Jean-Paul Sartre

For the existentialists, ethical considerations are paramount. Sartre could have been describing himself when he wrote of Albert Camus on the occasion of the latter's death that he represented the heritage of that long line of moralists whose works constitute what is perhaps most original in French letters. In Sartre's view, Camus's stubborn humanism reaffirmed the existence of moral fact against the opportunistic Machiavellians and the amoral 'realists' of his day.

Whether we consider Kierkegaard or Nietzsche, Heidegger or Jaspers, Sartre or de Beauvoir, Marcel or Camus, each in his or her own way was concerned with the 'moral fact'. The fact is that we are awash in obligations and values that are not the logical conclusion of any series of impersonal facts about the world. To paraphrase the philosopher David Hume (1711–76), no statements of fact can justify a statement of obligation without another statement of obligation having been previously introduced at least implicitly along the way. For example, if your conclusion is that someone ought not to murder, at least one of your reasons for the prohibition must have been the claim that murder belongs to the class of actions that ought not to be performed. One might reason that murder is the unjust taking of a human life with malice aforethought and that one ought not to perform unjust acts. Even if the list of reasons given is long, somewhere on that list is a command or a prohibition that turns the merely descriptive list into an obligation. As the well-worn argument concludes: The 'ought' of moral value or obligation cannot be derived from the 'is' of factual description by the mere linking of non-moral items. To the Nietzschean question 'Why be moral?' that could have been posed by Kierkegaard's aesthete as well, one cannot offer a non-moral answer such as 'it will make you happy'. Such a response would turn morality into an instrument for something else, in this case happiness, when, it is claimed, being moral is an end in itself. Kierkegaard's 'tragic hero', the Roman consul Brutus, for example, was probably not happy to have condemned his guilty son to death. This is often called the 'autonomy' of the moral realm. It is part of the Kantian heritage that the existentialists share – each in his or her own way, of course.

In Sartre's case, it is clear that the moral of the story is that there is always a moral to the story. Recall that he once confessed that his task was to give the bourgeoisie a bad conscience. Not that Sartre was a finger-wagging moralizer. Rather, he insisted that each of us acknowledges what we are doing with our lives right now. Like Kierkegaard's sea captain hesitating to come about while in the meantime the ship continues in its present direction, we are challenged to own up to our self-defining choices; to make them our own and consequently to become selves by acknowledging what we are. This is a form of Nietzsche's prescription to 'become what you are'. It's a matter of living the truth about ourselves, about our condition as human beings. The inauthentic person, in Sartre's view, is living a lie.

And what is that truth about our condition, and how are we to live it? Though it clearly involves a factual component, as we shall see, the truth which the authentic person lives is primarily a way of life, a manner of existing. In this regard, it resembles Kierkegaard's subjective truth, truth as appropriation, as 'making one's own', where the emphasis is on the how rather than on the what. But unlike subjective truth that concerns an objective uncertainty, Sartrean authenticity is grounded in a factual truth about the human condition even though this entails owning the way one intends to live the uncertainties of one's future.

But reference to the factual basis of authenticity brings us back to the basic question of humanism: What is the human being? What, if anything, distinguishes us from the rest of nature? We observed Heidegger distancing himself from the traditional responses to that question that he thought sold us short. And yet it is he who gave us the special use of the term 'authenticity' (*Eigentlich* in German, also translated as 'real' and etymologically as 'own' or 'proper'), which soon came to be perceived as the central existentialist virtue. Sartre admitted having borrowed the term from Heidegger. And though Heidegger insisted that the word and its converse, 'inauthentic', carried no moral significance, Sartre did not believe it. On the other hand, the related expressions 'good faith' and its converse 'bad faith' are Sartrean hallmarks that Sartre denied carried moral significance, though Heidegger asserted that they obviously did. In fact, both authors were mistaken, or better, each was unwilling to admit the moral uses to which these terms so easily lent themselves, whatever their originators' respective intentions.

Being-in-situation

As we sort out the existentialist truth of our condition and its ethical significance, let us begin with the existentialist insight that humans exist in-situation. Not only does this mean that we are not disembodied spirits floating above the material universe like birds winging their way across the water; to exist in-situation underscores that we are an integral part of that universe and the cultural world that envelops it. Less than angels, we are more than machines. Situation is an ambiguous mixture of what Sartre calls our 'facticity' and our 'transcendence'. 'Facticity' denotes the givens of our situation such as our race and nationality, our talents and limitations, the others with whom we deal as well as our previous choices. 'Transcendence' or the reach that our consciousness extends beyond these givens, denotes the takens of our situation, namely how we face up to this facticity. Transcendence functions somewhat like the 'intentionality' of consciousness, if we understand that term in a dynamic sense. Some born with a physical disability may meet the challenge in a positive, constructive manner while others may allow themselves to be crushed by the impairment. Sartre admits that the expression 'situation' is ambiguous in the sense that one cannot measure off the precise contribution of what is given and what is taken in each situation. For example, how much of my failure to succeed in becoming a surgeon is attributable to my lack of intelligence and physical skills or my deprived socioeconomic condition (facticity) and how much is due to my mental laziness and lack of discipline (transcendence)? But, as Simone de Beauvoir points out, from the very beginning, existentialism defined itself as a philosophy of ambiguity. These subjective and objective factors cannot be weighed and measured with precision. In fact, this ambiguity of the given and the taken pervades our individual and social lives. As Aristotle warned us, it is a mistake to seek a greater degree of clarity than the subject matter allows. You don't look for mathematical precision in moral matters. The existentialist applies this to life itself. To examine it in order to remove all ambiguity would resemble a silhouette-maker's approach to an impressionist painting. No one underscored that fundamental ambiguity of the human situation better than Merleau-Ponty, who was the philosopher of ambiguity *par excellence*.

What Heidegger calls our 'immersion' in the everyday world necessarily involves these two aspects. Recalling the essentially temporal dimension of human existence, one can describe this duality of facticity and transcendence as our ekstatic past and future respectively. Heidegger is the source of this threefold account of our ekstatic temporality, namely: 1) the past as facticity or 'thrownness' (we come on the scene not with a blank slate but already with a past); 2) the future as 'ek-sistence' or 'standing out' (we live in the 'not yet', the 'possible'); and 3) the present as immersion in the flood of our everyday concerns.

Of these three ekstatic dimensions, that of the future as the possible is most important. We are creatures of the 'possible'. Even the recovering alcoholic who tries to live life 'one day at a time' cannot avoid the spectre of the future. As Sartre remarks, the reformed gambler must renew his commitment every time he nears the gaming room. Existential anguish is our experience of the possible as the locus of our freedom. An old joke describes a man falling from the top of a very high building. As he speeds past the thirtieth floor, someone shouts 'How're you doin'?', 'So far so good!' is his optimistic reply. What is tragically laughable is this person's disregard for the dimension of the possible that is essential to his situation. That possibility is diminishing at the rate of gravity.

As I said at the outset, the existentialist personalizes the temporal as well as the spatial. Scientific space and time, such as Aristotle's conception of time as the measure of motion or Einstein's space-time continuum, are abstractions from the lived experience of existential space and time. If we did not have this original pre-metrical experience of the rush of time and the expanse of space, we would have nothing from which to abstract these scientific concepts. They would have no purchase on our lives. But whereas Heidegger uses these experiences to reveal the temporal horizon in which Being occurs (Being, for Heidegger, is not timeless), Sartre is more immediately intent on underscoring our responsibility for the necessarily ambiguous situation in which we live. Whatever our situation, it always includes the possibility of moving beyond it. As we said, the mantra of Sartrean humanism is that you can always make something out of what you've been made into because you always transcend your facticity.

Bifocal consciousness

Crucial to his notion of situation and of the self-deception that it makes possible is Sartre's understanding of consciousness as consisting of two aspects, the pre-reflective and the reflective. Fundamentally, consciousness is object-oriented (intentional) and translucent. It harbours no blind spots. As you read these words, you are aware of their meaning in the flow of the argument that you are following. You are pre-reflectively conscious of the argument. If someone interrupts with the question, 'What are you doing?', you can respond, now reflectively, 'I am (was) reading'. Though your consciousness was originally directed to the argument you were following, your reflective consciousness is now directed to a subject ('I') and an objective occurrence ('was reading'). Sartre's point is that the original, pre-reflective awareness was only implicitly (that is, non-positionally) self-aware; it was explicitly (positionally) aware of the argument on the page. Still, the subject was present, albeit 'in the wings', as it were, in the explicit awareness of the object, otherwise one could not have responded (reflectively) '"I" was reading'.

People are given general anaesthetics before an operation precisely to block their pre-reflective awareness in order to leave the reflective consciousness empty. In other words, the answer to the question 'What did you feel during the operation?' is supposed to be 'Nothing'. There is no conscious, pre-reflective 'experience' for the patient subsequently to reflect upon. As Sartre remarks: 'Every positional consciousness of an object is at the same time a non-positional consciousness of itself.' By appealing to an immediate, non-cognitive relation of the self to itself (non-positional self-consciousness), Sartre can assert that we are always implicitly 'self'-aware in every conscious act and that this self-awareness is occasionally made explicit by subsequent reflection. That is the difference between our responses to the two previous questions: I was implicitly self-aware as I consciously read the book; but I was not even implicitly self-aware when unconscious on the operating table.

The significance of this claim is both moral and cognitive. First, there need be no Freudian unconscious to underlie or shadow our conscious acts, compromising our responsibility. And, secondly, we can avoid the wild-goose chase of reflection on reflection to infinity in order to grasp the consciousness of self. *Every* conscious act is of its very nature self-aware, albeit implicitly so (that is, non-positionally). In a sense, this too underscores our responsibility. As Sartre insists, 'we are without excuse'.

If we take 'knowledge' to denote reflective awareness, we can say that we are aware of more than we know. Like the weak-willed dieter, we are pre-reflectively aware of our intention to take that second portion even as we (reflectively) protest to ourselves: 'I won't do this.' Sartre will later call this pre-reflective awareness 'comprehension' and insist that we comprehend more than we know. This in turn enables him to introduce a number of psychoanalytic terms into his account of the human condition without appeal to the unconscious, which, as mentioned, he thinks deprives us of our existential freedom. It is this bifocal nature of one and the same consciousness that makes self-deception possible without the aid of an unconscious.

Because we are fundamentally in-situation, and because this situation is as flowing and ambiguous as are time and consciousness themselves, humans are not stable, timeless identities. Whatever identity we have is either imposed from outside (which makes possible one form of bad faith, as we are about to see) or is sustained by our ongoing, self-defining existential project, our fundamental 'Choice'. It is this failure to coincide with ourselves that is the basis both of our freedom and of our capacity for self-deception. We are fundamentally a work in progress, a story in the process of being written. To deny this condition is to be in bad faith.

Bad faith

No existential category is better known in Sartrean existentialism than 'bad faith'. It certainly has wider usage in common parlance than 'good faith'. This is probably because, as a kind of self-deception, it is more widespread in its relevance. Heidegger argues that we are for the most part immersed in the average everyday where the inclination is to neglect our openness to Being and to simply 'go with the flow', that is, to live inauthentically as 'they' do. In an obvious allusion to the Biblical notion of Original Sin, Heidegger refers to this immersion as fallenness (*die Verfallenheit*). Sartre seems to agree that our usual inclination is to deny responsibility for our situation, that is, to be in bad faith. This is especially true in societies where exploitation and oppression are rampant, as he will later come to recognize. In fact, he claims that *Being and Nothingness* was a phenomenological study of individuals within an alienated society. Such societies foster self-deception about the structural injustices that our practices sustain. In these cases, even our protestation to be in good faith is a claim made in bad faith because it assumes that we can be in good faith the way a stone is a stone, that is, as completely identical with ourselves and free of responsibility, whereas we are always more than ourselves and hence without excuse. In other words, our temporalizing consciousness of what we are is always enough ahead of what we are that Sartre can claim that whatever we may be, we are in the manner of 'not-being' it. It is this gap which temporalizing consciousness introduces into our lives that accounts for our freedom and grounds our responsibility. It is also the source of that famous existential anguish (*Angst*) which denotes our implicit awareness of our freedom as the sheer possibility of possibility.

Inspired by Kierkegaard, the existentialist distinguishes anguish from fear. Whereas fear has a definite object, for example one is afraid of falling off a narrow precipice, anguish is the awareness that one could throw oneself off the ledge. It is the awareness that any choice is within our power to make, even if its success may elude us. But despite its often abstract language, existentialism, as we saw, aims to be a concrete philosophy. The possibilities to which it refers, even the possibility with no specific object – the sheer awareness of freedom – denotes the consciousness of *my* situated freedom and possibility. As Sartre puts it, 'The recruit who reports for active duty at the beginning of the war can in some instances be afraid of death, but more often he is "afraid of being afraid"; that is, he is filled with anguish before himself.'

The 'faith' of bad faith

Before moving to the two basic forms of bad faith, let us note what Sartre calls the 'faith' of bad faith because it both reveals his exceedingly high standard for what constitutes 'evidence' and provides the key to bad faith as the choice to be satisfied with 'non-persuasive' evidence. Briefly, Sartre adopts a roughly phenomenological, evidential view of knowledge as the immediate presence to consciousness of the object itself. As we saw in Chapter 1, the intentional nature of consciousness places us immediately in the world without the need for ideas in the mind that we presume resemble what is found in the 'external' world. He distinguishes between the 'certain' and the 'probable', depending on whether this object is grasped reflectively in an immediate 'self-evident' intuition, the way one gets the point of a mathematical demonstration or catches one's spouse in *flagrante delicto* or, on the contrary, whether the object pursued is merely indicated by something else that is evidence for or against its presence, as when trying to confirm a scientific hypothesis or noticing lipstick on his shirt collar. In the former cases, one has the object itself adequately present; in the latter, one has clues or evidence for the object which itself is not yet evident, that is, not yet confirmed. Sartre's thesis is that belief in general is the attitude that relies on evidence of the latter kind whereas knowledge requires the immediate grasp of the thing itself – a very high standard, indeed, for what counts as knowledge. Such faith is 'good' in the epistemic sense if it limits itself to persuasive evidence, and 'bad' if it settles in advance on insufficient evidence. Bad faith, he claims, is the spontaneous ordering of one's life to settle on non-persuasive evidence. Once one has 'fallen in love' with a particular person, for example, one may search for evidence in support of the 'decision' and intentionally, albeit pre-reflectively, neglect evidence to the contrary even though one's friends might question what one finds attractive about that person. As Sartre describes it: 'One puts oneself in bad faith as one goes to sleep and one is in bad faith as one dreams.' But because of the unblinking eye of pre-reflective consciousness, one is aware of having settled for this non-persuasive evidence. One remains responsible for remaining in bad faith.

Two forms of bad faith

It is flight from the anguish of our freedom that motivates our bad faith, and it is the duality of the human condition as both facticity and transcendence that makes bad faith possible. Bad faith is the attempt to escape the tension of this duality by denying one of its poles. Accordingly, Sartre speaks of two forms of bad faith. The more common form tries to collapse our transcendence (our possibility) into our facticity (our antecedent condition). In effect, one flees responsibility by claiming: 'That's just the way I am.' The various forms of determinism from the Marxist economic to Freudian psychological variety provide theoretical versions of this basic form of bad faith. They relieve us of the anguish of our freedom by denying that we are free in this creative, existentialist sense. This type of bad faith is resigned to the pattern of life laid out in advance and over which one has no control and hence is free of responsibility. It would be the opposite of the creative 'choice' of Camus's Sisyphus or of Dylan Thomas's advice to his dying father:

Do not go gentle into that good night.
Rage, rage against the dying of the light.

Both the novelist and the poet intensify the awareness and

responsibility of the agent. Again, these examples of authenticity are versions of Nietzsche's transformation of the 'it was' into the 'I willed it so'. The deterministic form of bad faith, on the other hand, counsels dull resignation to one's fate. As we noted earlier, this is the basis of Sartre's denial of the Freudian unconscious. Still, as we observed, he retains many 'Freudian' insights by appealing to our 'pre-theoretical' comprehension of our acts that precede our explicit, reflective awareness. And it is in the 'unity' of this tensive consciousness that the self-deception occurs. For, paradoxically, one could not 'lie' to oneself if one were not divided in some basic sense; yet if one were completely other than the one deceived, we would not have self-deception but a case of what Sartre calls the 'cynical lie'. Bad faith is as paradoxical as consciousness itself. In Sartre's words, bad faith is 'knowledge that is ignorant and ignorance that knows better'. And this occurs within the unity of one and the same implicit self-consciousness.

Another version of this collapse of transcendence (possibility) is the attitude of bad faith which allows another subject to determine the 'identity' to which we try to conform. This version is rooted in our interpersonal relations, in what Sartre calls our 'being-for-others'. Sartre's example of the perfect waiter is a case in point. The man's movement is quick and studied. He is a bit too solicitous for the customer's order. He returns balancing his tray recklessly yet giving the impression of complete control, and so forth. Sartre observes that he is playing at *being* a waiter in a cafe. He has become the slave to an image that others' expectations have imposed upon him and which he has appropriated. Bad faith enters when the agent dismisses any other kind of behaviour as inconceivable. He simply 'is' a waiter with his entire being, the way a stone is a stone. But his consciousness makes such total identity impossible. Pre-reflectively, he is aware of the game but reflectively, he has focused on the job to be done in this particular way and chosen to overlook his sustaining project of excluding other possibilities. On the other hand, to choose to live the anguish of continuously renewing this project with the full realization that at any moment one could shed the apron and leave the profession would be a form of good faith. But owning such freedom and the anguish it entails is usually avoided.

The second, less common form of bad faith consists in discounting our antecedent condition in sheer wishfulness, as if we were pure possibility with no actuality, living entirely in the future, unencumbered by any past. This is the bad faith of the dreamer as exemplified in James Thurber's character 'Walter Mitty'. Walter is a daydreamer incapable of connecting with the real world. Any occurrence can set him to fantasizing about the hero he would like to be, when, in fact, his life is unadventurous and commonplace. So too, the student who insists that she is going to become a brain surgeon but who automatically reaches for the snooze button on her alarm rather than get out of bed to attend her chemistry class is acting in bad faith. Like the sea captain, again, she has chosen not to choose, which is to say that she has (pre-reflectively) chosen not to be that surgeon but without (reflectively) acknowledging the fact. She is deceiving herself. She is living in bad faith.

Both forms of bad faith adhere to a falsehood about the human condition, insisting that it is either transcendence or facticity when, in fact, it is both but in an ambiguous mix that those who cannot bear to live in ambiguity find unnerving. But those who accept the challenge to live this truth about their condition are what Sartre calls 'authentic'.

Existing authentically

We spoke of the existentialist project of becoming an individual. Authenticity is a feature of the existentialist individual. In fact, existential individuality and authenticity seem to imply one another. One is no more born an individual (in the existentialist sense) than is one born authentic. To be truly authentic is to have realized one's individuality and vice versa. Both existential 'individuality' and 'authenticity' are achievement words. The person who avoids choice, who becomes a mere face in the crowd or cog in the bureaucratic machine, has failed to become authentic. So we can now describe the person who lives his or her life as 'they' command or expect as being inauthentic.

Tolstoy's main character in *The Death of Ivan Ilyich* for most of his life is inauthentic. When he finally comes to embrace his impending death rather then resignedly letting it happen, he becomes authentic. The move from recognizing the death that 'they' die as humans to acknowledging the death that bears my name is a step towards authenticity. For Heidegger, the temporal dimension of the future as the possible takes precedence over the dimension of the past as facticity, though neither can be ignored in assessing the authenticity of *Dasein*. He argues that my being-unto-death, my mortal temporality, is my most proper possibility because it is the end of my other possibilities and, for Heidegger, possibility is the most important of the three dimensions of ekstatic temporality. On this view, inauthenticity consists in fleeing our mortality by diluting it into an event that happens to everyone. As Ivan Ilyich protests:

> The syllogism he had learnt from Kiesewetter's Logic: 'Caius is a man, men are mortal, therefore Caius is mortal,' had always seemed to him correct as applied to Caius, but certainly not as applied to himself. That Caius – man in the abstract – was mortal, was perfectly correct, but he was not Caius, not an abstract man, but a creature quite, quite separate from all others. . . . Caius really was mortal, and it was right for him to die; but for me, little Vanya, Ivan Ilych, with all my thoughts and emotions, it's altogether a different matter. It cannot be that I ought to die. That would be too terrible.

For Heidegger, it is the resolute acceptance of one's being-unto-death that funnels our otherwise scattered concerns into the realization of what it means to be. This is another way of experiencing our contingency. Once we realize that at some point in time we will no longer be, we gain some insight into what it means to exist. Even if we believe in personal immortality, the entry into that 'good night' is not free of risk, as Marcel realized.

And as Moses Herzog observes, 'this is how we teach metaphysics on each other'.

Sartre differs from Heidegger in that he considers 'my death' foreign to my experience. Yes, I can observe another's dying and imagine myself in that condition, but that is as far as it goes. My death is what Sartre calls an 'unrealizable' because it lies just beyond the threshold of my experience, a lesson he doubtless learned from Epicurus (341–270 BC). And yet he too links authenticity with the unity of a life. In his case, however, it is the self-defining Choice or project that brings the multiplicity of our concerns into a whole and invites our authentic embrace.

Whether we realize it reflectively or not, Sartre believes that fundamental Choice (which I shall capitalize so as to distinguish it from those other decisions and selections designated 'choices' that we make under this life-guiding Choice) is the unifying meaning and direction (the French word '*sens*' denotes both) of our lives. In this fundamental sense, Choice is pre-reflective. It is what we are and not just what we do. We come to reflective consciousness having already made this Choice. Its concrete expressions are the many choices (small 'c') that articulate this project.

Sartre argues that our original Choice is our futile pursuit of being consciously self-identical. We have seen that the quest for identity is on a collision course with our consciousness as *non*-self-identical. Yet most of us act as if we could attain the solidity and identity of things; that we could be conscious things. This is the impossible ideal of divinity, he protests, and our pursuit of it expresses an inauthentic flight from the anguish of our own freedom. Ours is the freedom of *non*-self-identity. Whatever we are, whether waiter or soldier or woman on a date, to mention three of his examples, we possess each quality in the manner of 'othering' it; that is, in the manner of a conscious subject. If any of these features characterizes us in our own eyes or in the eyes of others, we sustain them in the manner of being somewhat beyond them; we are responsible for the way we sustain these qualities. In Sartre's dramatic phrase, 'we are condemned to be free'.

But if, for the most part, people seek the security of being identical with their roles in life or with what others expect of them, even though the anguish of their repressed freedom cannot be entirely squelched, each person articulates his or her existential Choice in a particular manner in accord with the facticity of their situation. Sartre believes that 'human reality' is a totality, not a loose collection. Again, we are a story in the making and not a disconnected set of events merely juxtaposed. It is this life-defining Choice or 'project' that unifies our experiences and the multiplicity of options that follow upon this Choice.

It follows that one should be able to discover a person's signature way of trying to coincide with themselves by reviewing the individual choices (small 'c') that describe their life up to this point. Sartre calls this interpretation of such choices to reveal the fundamental Choice 'existential psychoanalysis'. Such psychoanalysis makes no appeal to a freedom-extinguishing unconscious, but, Sartre concedes, it has yet to find its Freud. And while he admits the possibility of a 'radical conversion' wherein one would 'Choose' to live the anguished existence of an authentic freedom without seeking self-identity, such fundamental changes in life-direction are rare.

Still, exceptional or not, an ethic of authenticity such as Sartre promised in a footnote to *Being and Nothingness* is possible. Anyone seeking its details, from Sartre's perspective, would do well to read his posthumously published *Notebooks for an Ethics*. There they will find Sartre venturing hypotheses, noting insights, and sketching the elements for a moral philosophy that he never formulated as a whole. This is a far cry from the coffee-table existentialist exhibited in *Being and Nothingness*. Sign of a radical conversion? Rather, it provides a glimpse of the positive side of existentialist ethics that would emerge once the 'alienated society' described phenomenologically in the earlier book had been dismantled.

Frequently dramatized in the imaginative form that the topic invites, the existentialist view of the human being is that he or she is permeated with contingency, as Roquentin experienced in *Nausea*. Like the Heideggerian in the face of personal mortality or the Nietzschean 'free spirit' who courageously welcomes the infinite repetition of the past, the authentic individual, on Sartre's account, is the one who embraces this contingency and lives it fully.

An ethics of authenticity

Authenticity is often seen as an ethical gyroscope serving to help one keep one's bearings in a state of Nietzschean moral free-fall. If the authentic person is ethically 'creative' and has ventured out beyond the last lighthouse of ethical security; if, like Kierkegaard's Abraham or Nietzsche's free spirit, the agent has suspended the traditional ethical rules with their appeal to the universal based on the maxim 'what if everybody did that?' in favour of the unique, the unprecedented, the situational, then to what criteria can one appeal to warrant the claim to be playing the ethical game at all? It would seem that so-called moral creativity is a cover for nihilism, or at least a mask for sheer opportunism. And yet we have claimed that the existentialists hold ethical considerations paramount. What kind of ethics can they possibly be proposing?

It has been suggested that what existentialists offer us in the long run is more an ethical *style* than a moral content. They may counsel us how to live but, as de Beauvoir insisted, they do not offer us moral recipes. This is not an unwarranted claim. Nietzsche certainly emphasized the importance of style over substance, which he dismissed as shopworn metaphysics. He counselled that those capable of bearing such advice should make of their lives a work of art. And Sartre likened moral choice to the construction of a work of art in the sense that neither art nor moral choice were subject to strict rules. But, unlike Nietzsche and closer to Kierkegaard, Sartre acknowledged a 'universal' character to moral judgements. De Beauvoir remarks that 'an ethics of ambiguity will be one which will refuse to deny *a priori* that separate existents can, at the same time, be bound to each other, that their individual freedoms can forge laws valid for all'. In fact, she goes on to emphasize 'the importance of that universal, absolute end which freedom itself is'.

Freedom constitutes the ultimate value for the existentialists just as authenticity is their primary virtue. But, as de Beauvoir points out, this is not the empty freedom of indifference (where 'anything goes'), yet neither is it the 'freedom' under the rule-bound 'serious man' who submerges his freedom under the dictates of society. Like Nietzsche, she finds the roots of nihilism in the failure of such a spirit of seriousness. As people come to reject the strict moral categories of religious or philosophical tradition, they end up rejecting any ultimate values at all, a position called 'nihilism'. But those, on the contrary, who feel the joy of existence and assume its gratuity (that is, those who joyfully embrace their contingency), she suggests, will weather the nihilistic storm brought on by Nietzsche's 'death of God'. In other words, the 'content' of existential choice is freedom itself made concrete by the embrace of its radical contingency, its lack of self-coincidence. Again, whatever I am, I am in the manner of not-being it; that is, of not being limited to it and of consciously extending beyond it.

But does this not devolve into a mere style of life, after all? Does it matter what one 'embraces' freely so long as one embraces something? If the joyous embrace of one's contingency is what 'authenticity' means, could one not be an authentic anti-Semite or Nazi? De Beauvoir argues that the real requirement of an individual's freedom is that it pursues what she calls 'an open future' by seeking to extend itself by means of the freedom of others. In other words, my freedom is enhanced, not diminished, when I work to expand the freedom of others. This is her elaboration of Sartre's claim, mentioned in Chapter 3, that my concrete freedom requires that, in choosing, I choose the freedom of others. And 'freedom' in this concrete sense means the pursuit of the 'open future' of others, that is, the maximization of their possibilities as well as my own. On this account, it would be 'inauthentic' to leave others in slavery or a state of oppression, much less to enslave them, for, as de Beauvoir explains, a freedom wills itself authentically only by willing itself as an indefinite movement through the freedom of others.

So while existential authenticity does have a content, namely the willing of freedom both for oneself and for all others, the meaning of that freedom has yet to be analysed. It became the task of existentialists to do so as they faced the problem of concrete freedom and social ethics.

Chapter 5

A chastened individualism? Existentialism and social thought

In history too, existence precedes essence.

Jean-Paul Sartre

It may be shameful to be happy by oneself.

Albert Camus, *The Plague*

When Sartre entered the lecture hall on that October evening of 1945, he was facing the widespread belief that his newly popular philosophy was simply a warmed-up version of bourgeois individualism, totally insensitive to the mortal camaraderie that had just defeated Fascism across the continent. This suspicion was confirmed by the often-quoted penultimate line of his play *No Exit*, 'Hell is other people' (*L'enfer c'est les autres*), that was premiered the year before. The outburst of Sartre's creativity that followed the liberation of Paris seemed to reinforce the implicit narcissism of his ethic of authenticity and critique of bad faith, neither of which addressed pressing social issues. This was certainly the view of both his Communist and his Catholic critics, well represented at that lecture, both of whom championed explicit, if mutually incompatible, theories of social justice and programmes to implement them. And yet what we have been calling the existentialist tradition, notwithstanding its stress on becoming an individual, was uniformly critical of bourgeois society with its penchant for conformity and material comfort, its pursuit of security and aversion to risk, and its unimaginative conservatism. But does this translate into a full-blown social theory, especially one that recognizes exploitation and oppression and advocates their termination? I'll respond by examining the respective answers of the leading members of that tradition.

Kierkegaard and Nietzsche on bourgeois culture

I pointed out earlier that Kierkegaard is noted for his polemics against the three formative institutions of Danish society in his day, namely Hegelian philosophy, the established Church, and the popular press. Hegelian philosophy, in his view, had traded life for concept (*Begriff*). He agreed with what was then the dominant school of thought in Denmark that life was to be understood 'historically' in the sense that the Hegelian system could uncover the necessities of events after they had occurred. But he insisted that such speculation was powerless before the contingencies of life as it is lived.

> It is perfectly true, as philosophers say, that life must be understood backwards. But they forget the other proposition, that it must be lived forwards.
>
> (*Journals*, 1843)

Ideas can be systematized, life cannot. Attempting to live your life by relying on abstract, Hegelian philosophy, Kierkegaard scoffed, is like taking your laundry to a shop that announces 'Washing Done' and discovering that only the sign is for sale!

But the established Lutheran Church did not fare any better. Undertaking the project of reintroducing Biblical 'Christianity' into 'Christendom', Kierkegaard identified the latter with a cultural Christianity that promoted complacency, greed, and tokenism towards the poor and suffering while profiting from its identification with the political and economic powers of the day. He noted that the State employs a thousand officials (the clergy) who, while professing Christianity, in fact are interested only in their incomes and actually prevent people from knowing what Christianity truly is. Though his brother was a pastor and Søren himself had considered entering the ministry, his particular religiosity placed him at loggerheads with the established Church.

And then there was the popular press. Kierkegaard considered it a demoralizing institution. It undermines the courageous search for the truth and instead serves the formation of public opinion, the view of the many who do not wish to risk possible exclusion from the majority that thinking for themselves entails. He paid dearly for such remarks by the ridicule he suffered at the hands of one satirical weekly in particular, the *Corsair*. Its caricatures made him the laughing-stock of Copenhagen, such that he hesitated to take his beloved walks around the city.

As for the bourgeoisie in general, he wrote that, for them, morality ranks highest, much more important than intelligence; but they've never felt that fervour for the great, the talented, even in an exceptional guise. Their *morals* are a brief summary of the various posters put out by the police; the most important thing is to be a useful member of the State, and to air their opinions in the club of an evening; they never feel that nostalgia for something unknown, something remote, never feel the depths of being nothing at all (*Journals*, 14 July 1837).

Each of these remarks could have been made by Nietzsche. Both men prized a brutal honesty and had a sensitive nose for cowardice and hypocrisy. Each appealed to the Socratic willingness to be persecuted for the sake of the truth. And they both wrote with such wit and vigour.

As I pointed out in Chapter 2, much of the foregoing is voiced in support of the 'individual', which accounts for Kierkegaard's reputation as elitist and apolitical. That he was distrustful of revolutions and of the mobs that often carried them out is quite clear. And if his wry humour did not spare the monarchy or the aristocrats, this should not be taken as a sign of egalitarian leanings. Rather, Kierkegaard maintained the kind of conservatism in which sceptical attitudes often take refuge. In this sense, his 'individualism' represents the point of departure for our attempt to trace the career of a social conscience in the existentialist tradition.

But before turning to Nietzsche, the other figure at this initial stage, we should note that Kierkegaard's Christianity, the very ideal from which he attacked 'Christendom', was clearly sensitive to the plight of the poor and oppressed. His criticism of ecclesiastical politics and functionaries was grounded in 'Gospel values'. Rightly or wrongly, his critique of the State Church focused on its having compromised these values in practice while proclaiming them in word. But in a vintage year for European revolutions (1848), including one taking place outside the very window of his study while he was correcting page proofs for his next publication, Kierkegaard seemed more concerned about the inner life; more focused on promoting a merciful attitude both towards and on the part of the needy, than about the social injustices that motivated their revolutionary behaviour. To be sure, his contrast between the age of revolution as being essentially passionate and the present age as 'essentially a sensible, reflecting age, devoid of passion, flaring up in superficial, short-lived enthusiasm and prudentially relaxing in indolence' would count as a social psychological critique. And if his rhetoric carries him up to the barricades, as in the remark that 'in contrast to the age of revolution, which took action, the present age is an age of publicity, the age of miscellaneous announcements: nothing happens but still there is instant publicity', his sceptical wit draws him back. Thus, he could insist that a chapter in his *Works of Love* (1847) on 'Mercifulness' was written in direct opposition to Communism. Change of heart rather than social upheaval seems to have been his preferred solution; personal conversion rather than political revolution.

Nietzsche was equally distrustful of the 'herd'. And his disdain for political democracy matched Kierkegaard's. His attitudes were scarcely mollified or, he would claim, distracted by appeal to Gospel values, which he had systematically inverted on several occasions. Pity, to pick a close associate of Kierkegaard's 'mercy', for example, he dismissed as demeaning of its object and unworthy of its subject. In effect, Nietzsche seems to have shared Kierkegaard's concern with the attitude or spirit of individuals rather than with the socioeconomic conditions under which they laboured. And while his 'higher types' were Greek or, like Goethe, figures of high culture whereas Kierkegaard's heroes are chiefly Biblical in inspiration, neither addressed the issue of social responsibility or other major topics in political philosophy except in passing. Like Kierkegaard, Nietzsche was more concerned with the formation of individuals than with the transformation of society. In this sense, the existentialist tradition had yet to face what came to be known in the 19th century as the social question, namely how to achieve an equitable distribution of the growing wealth and services of industrial societies in the face of a burgeoning proletariat.

Heidegger and Jaspers: being-with and the lure of National Socialism

If Nietzsche was disturbed by the dark cloud of nihilism that he saw enveloping European society at the realization of the 'death of God', Heidegger and other German intellectuals of his generation were more concerned with the rise of Bolshevism and the threat of its hordes to Western civilization. Equally menacing, though more subtle in its insinuation, was the crass materialism and technologism of Anglo-American capitalism. German culture, as heir apparent to that of Ancient Greece (a view propounded in Germany by distinguished 18th- and 19th-century Classical philologists and archaeologists), was under attack from two directions and at two levels in what Heidegger in a lecture called 'great pincers, squeezed between Russia on one side and America on the other'.

Despite the individualizing power of resolutely accepting one's personal being-unto-death, Heidegger spoke of our being-with (*Mitzein*) as a basic structure of human being (*Dasein*). Humans are fundamentally social in nature. We are originally born (in the language of ekstatic temporality, Heidegger says 'thrown') into a cultural world where our being-with conforms to what 'anyone' does. We develop what sociologists call a 'social self' and what Heidegger denominates an inauthentic 'they' self (*Das Man*) like that of Ivan Ilyich, in thrall to public opinion. From a historical point of view, this cultural world is what Heidegger calls 'tradition', etymologically that which has been 'handed down' and which we have received as part of our common heritage. This tradition helps form us as a people. He sometimes speaks of 'destiny' in this context, meaning not blind fate but the objective limits and possibilities that emerge out of our collective past. In the existentialist sense, these possibilities can be taken as opportunities for authentic or inauthentic choice.

But there are historical moments that occasion the emergence of an authentic being-with and Heidegger (mis)read the National Socialist (Nazi) revolution as one of them. As a biographer whom I consider fair-minded summarizes this controversial matter:

> A good deal of uneasiness persists to this day about Heidegger's political involvement. On philosophical grounds he became, for a while, a National Socialist revolutionary, but his philosophy also helped him to free himself from the political scene. He learned a lesson from what he had done, and his thinking subsequently focused on the problem of the seducibility of the spirit by the will to power.

Though existentialists tend toward nonconformity and Heidegger, as we saw, emphasized the individualizing power of resolutely living 'my' being-unto-death, the notion of 'authentic' *being-with* proved as perilous as it was alluring. Heidegger seemed seduced by the sheer power of the Nazi movement and the opportunity it seemed to offer for educational reform in which he might play an important role. What philosopher Jürgen Habermas (1929–   ) said of Heidegger has often been applied to Sartre in this regard: that by making the individual the focal point of their philosophies they overlooked the intersubjective and social aspect of human life. Though an inaccurate assessment of both Heidegger and Sartre, such criticism nonetheless underscores the fact that the burden of proof for an adequate social philosophy rests with such proponents of the authentic individual.

If the Second World War ended with Heidegger in disgrace, it left Karl Jaspers standing on the moral high ground. Although Jaspers too had believed that the cultural mission of Germany was to offer the world a third option between 'the Russian whip and Anglo-Saxon convention', he voiced this opinion after the First World War and, unlike Heidegger, not in the midst of the Nazi triumph. He had withstood the Nazi takeover at the cost of his university professorship and at the end of the war delivered a set of lectures published as *The Question of German Guilt* (1947). There he distinguished forms of guilt and responsibility in order to clarify how the Germans should sort out their present situation in the wake of this disaster. He discerned four categories of guilt: criminal guilt (the violation of unambiguous laws), political guilt (the degree of political acquiescence in the actions of the Nazi regime), moral guilt (a matter of personal conscience formed in dialogue with one's ethical community), and metaphysical guilt (based on the solidarity of all humans simply as human and resulting in a condition of co-responsibility, especially for injustices of which one is aware and which one does not do one's best to resist). This sense of collective responsibility was new to existentialist thought, but the topic would soon be addressed by Sartre in his polemics with various exploitative and oppressive groups and societies. Years later, Sartre would be inspired by these lectures to write a play, *The Condemned of Altona* (1959), that, while ostensibly portraying the responsibility of the Germans for the Second World War, was actually a parable of

French guilt in repressing the Algerian revolution under way at that time.

The experience of the Second World War and its aftermath was decisive for Jaspers as it would be for Sartre. The abiding ethical concern of existentialist thought surfaces in Jaspers's appeal to the ethical as a limit to the political. He will have no truck with the crass Machiavellian amoral 'realism' which claims that the end justifies the means. Jaspers's experience with the Nazis had driven that point home, if he had ever questioned it. But the advent of the atomic bomb had multiplied the stakes exponentially. Sounding like Kierkegaard yet with a sense of institutional change as well, Jaspers remarks that it is not enough to find new institutions; we must change ourselves, our characters, our moral-political wills. What has been present in the individual person for a long time already, what was effective in small groups but remained powerless in society as a whole, has now become the condition for the continued existence of mankind.

Several years earlier, Gabriel Marcel had voiced a similar fear when he observed that we are in a situation without precedent in which suicide has become possible on a mankind-wide scale. It is impossible to think out this situation, he insists, without becoming aware that each of us is at almost every moment in the presence of a radical choice, and contributes by what he thinks, by what he does, by what he is, either to increase or, on the contrary, to lessen the likelihood of such a world-scale suicide. But he believes that it is only at the philosophical level that the essential nature of this choice can be made clear and that is what he proceeds to do. Existentialism demands a social conscience. But the particular urgency of its demand is a response to what he takes to be a fact unprecedented in world history: our capability of effecting the total destruction of civilization as we know it.

In the existentialist manner, Jaspers is not proposing another ethic of rules, despite his admission that a 'form' of universality remains in place, namely the unconditioned 'ought' of moral obligation. For the content of this obligation, 'what' specifically I ought to do, he insists, cannot be deduced from the form of the unconditional obligation to do something. Of course, good must be done and evil avoided; I 'ought' to do my duty. But what is my duty here and now? What is the good that I ought to pursue in this situation? As Jaspers knew from experience, such discovery/creation demands the courage of sacrifice on the part of the ethical agent as well as a form of reason that is more than intellect. Ethos, Jaspers warns us, becomes morality when it exhausts itself in commands and prohibitions. And here his theistic commitment comes into play: 'What is hidden in the ethical', he assures us, 'is more than merely ethical.' It is 'transcendent', and even 'divine', but not religious in the common use of the term that denotes revealed religion and institutional authority. As did Kierkegaard and Nietzsche, each in his own way, Jaspers leaves us open to the risk of moral creativity but does so within the horizon of the transcendent, or what he calls the 'encompassing' that challenges us to realize our freedom in a manner that entails the utmost responsibility for the freedom of others.

The challenge of mass society: Marcel

Though Jaspers called his thought a 'philosophy of *Existenz*', it seems to have been Gabriel Marcel who coined the term 'existentialist' and applied it to Sartre. His preferred label for his own work was 'neo-Socratic'. Like Socrates, Marcel is an outspoken critic of contemporary society. And like him, he is a courageous defender of truth in the face of the will-to-power or, for that matter, the will-to-truth – which Nietzsche had criticized as an unacknowledged form of will-to-power.

In a book published in 1951, the title of which epitomizes an existentialist social critique, *Man against Mass Society*, Marcel moves beyond the neo-Romantic disdain for industrial society and its technological heirs, with which existentialists are commonly associated, to address the standard existentialist themes of freedom, the specificity of the human, the crisis of values, and ethical authenticity. But at Marcel's hands, each of these themes takes on an openly social character, mounted in a critique of totalitarianism on the one hand and of materialism on the other. Its underlying thesis is a relentless struggle against what he calls the 'spirit of abstraction'. This spirit, for example, figures necessarily in our declaring and sustaining war. Whether it is a matter of attacking the enemy, usually demonized with insulting epithets, or of launching missiles, the human consequences of which one does not witness, one is spared the painful experience of the concrete reality of one's actions. This point is brought home with rhetorical force in the pacifist film *All Quiet on the Western Front*, in which the abstraction of fighting the enemy is played out against the concrete reality of trench warfare during the First World War. Marcel's criticism of the spirit of abstraction is a continuance of the search for a concrete philosophy that captured the interest of many philosophers and led Sartre to phenomenology in the 1930s.

Politically, Marcel finds the spirit of abstraction at work in the fanaticism of what he calls the 'masses'. As he explains, the present political situation leaves large numbers of people in a state of abasement and alienation. They lack a sense of their own worth and are strangers to themselves and one another. The result is that the masses are inevitably prone to fanaticism: propaganda has the convulsive effect of electrical shock on people in this state. The philosopher, he claims, must work for a social order that will free as many as possible from such a mass condition.

He goes on to offer a phenomenological description of 'fanaticized' consciousness. Mass society is Marcel's version of Nietzsche's 'herd'. Its members can be trained but not educated. And yet, unlike Nietzsche, Marcel urges that social and political steps can be taken to 'draw' such beings out of their state of abasement and alienation. His solution is more 'communitarian' than 'liberal' in today's terms. That is, it favours intermediate groups as in the ancient guild system to mediate and control the absolutist tendencies of the State.

The operative term is 'communion', which, in his vocabulary, signifies mutual respect among members of a group who share a common interest and concern. It is not unlike what Sartre at about the same time was calling 'fraternity'.

The basis of this liberation is the move from abstract to concrete thinking. Humans are essentially in a situation of one sort or another, but this is what an abstract kind of humanism tends to overlook. This is what Sartre was saying in his humanism lecture: if we are to pursue freedom in the concrete rather than merely dream of it in the abstract, he insists, we must address the alienated situation of others. We cannot be free until they too have been liberated. Such is the argument of his 'Is Existentialism a Humanism?' lecture. But as Sartre said of the anti-Semite, we cannot act directly on another freedom; we must deal with their condition; we must change the 'bases and structures' of their choice. Marcel would agree with Sartre that such bases and structures cannot be simply economic or mechanically materialistic. But he would join Jaspers in insisting that the true value of the human lies in his or her ability to move beyond their condition towards openness to the transcendent. Fostering such receptiveness helps curb the totalitarian tendencies of the modern State and opens up the dogmatism of ethical systems.

Sartre and Camus on the Algerian war

Sartre claimed that his experience as a conscript in the Second World War brought him out of his individualism and led to his discovery of society. Merleau-Ponty recalls being struck by the extent to which during the pre-war years Sartre was removed from the political and historical point of view. It was only in the early days after the liberation of France that he became involved in politics. First, in the non-Communist politics of the Left, but as the Cold War developed, he shared political and social concerns with his former critics, the French Communist Party (PCF). Though he never joined the Party, he maintained a love-hate relationship with the PCF until the Hungarian Revolution (1956), when it started to weaken, and the Soviet occupation of Prague (1962), when the positive relationship died completely.

Sartre was at heart a political anarchist (what the French called a 'libertarian socialist') in the sense that he thought all relations should be voluntary and egalitarian. He described authority as 'the other in us' and was suspicious of its every form. But he was also a moralist, meaning that his political involvements always carried a moral dimension. Merleau-Ponty once said that if you distinguish acts of oppression from impersonal structures of exploitation, Sartre always focused on the act rather than on the structural dimension of the problem at hand. That is where the moral responsibility lay. Not that he ignored what philosopher Louis Althusser called 'structural causality', he did not. But these social structures, he insisted, were the sedimentation of prior actions and are sustained by current actions. So when, for example, he describes colonialism as a 'system', and says the 'meanness is in the system', he means that it is an exploitative structure that demands and is kept alive by oppressive practices. In other words, the 'meanness' is not entirely in the system. In principle, one should be able to discover the responsible parties, to name names. That's a basic existentialist assumption.

It was this 'naming of names' with respect to the French involvement in quelling the Algerian revolution that placed Sartre on a collision course with his friend Albert Camus. Born in Algeria of a French father and Spanish mother, Camus was active in the Resistance movement during the Nazi occupation. As editor of its clandestine paper, *Combat*, he was sought by the Gestapo. With modest training in philosophy, he was primarily a journalist and an actor. Sartre's enthusiastic review of his early novel *The Outsider* led to their meeting and eventual friendship. In fact, Sartre offered him the male lead in *No Exit*, which Camus considered but declined because of the need to maintain a low profile under the occupation.

Despite having written articles in support of the Arab population in

11. Albert Camus, the newspaper, and the city

Albert Camus (1913–60)

Born in Algeria of Alsatian and Spanish parentage, his father died in the First World War and he was raised in poverty by his widowed mother. In Algeria, he was active in theatre and journalism before moving in 1940 to Paris, where he soon became involved in the Resistance movement, editing the clandestine newspaper *Combat*. His first novel, *The Outsider*, as well as an essay, 'The Myth of Sisyphus', both published in 1942, made him famous and brought him to the attention of Jean-Paul Sartre. He soon became associated with the existentialist movement. He received the Nobel Prize for Literature in 1957 and died in a car accident in 1960.

Algeria, one of the reasons for his need to move to metropolitan France, Camus thought the Arabs should not be deprived of such benefits of French citizenship as its educational system that had enabled a poor youth like himself to escape poverty. He also viewed the revolution as the expression of a pan-Arab expansionism, led by Egypt. Between the extremes of the status quo and complete revolution, Camus counselled some kind of federation. In other words, this author of *The Rebel* recommended the middle road. Sartre, seldom given to moderation or compromise, especially in politics, came down strongly in favour of the revolution, so much so that reactionary groups exploded bombs at the entrance to his apartment building on two occasions. As Sartre slipped into what he would later call a period of 'amoral realism', in support of revolution wherever he deemed it necessary, Camus attended more and more to the ethical aspect of political and social upheaval, opposing capital punishment and espousing a kind of pacifism by the time of his accidental death at the age of 47.

It was the savaging of Camus's book *The Rebel* by a close associate of Sartre's in the journal that Sartre directed that brought this friendship to an end. But the break was inevitable. Sartre took his politics more seriously than he took his friendships, as we shall see in the case of Merleau-Ponty as well. As Sartre's politics moved increasingly towards the Left, he separated himself from former friends whose political development moved in the opposite direction. By the time of the student revolt of 1968, Sartre was associating with so-called French 'Maoists' who had little to do with China but a great deal to do with such classical anarchist ideals as 'direct democracy'. Sartre could now publish an essay entitled 'The Communists Are Afraid of Revolution'. This marks the extreme of Sartre's political existentialism.

Recent discussions have polished Camus's image in this affair. He emerges as the more balanced and less polemical of the two. But nothing in the episode speaks for the fairness or tolerance of either party.

12. Franz (France) assuming full responsibility for the atrocities of the war (in Sartre's play *The Condemned of Altona*)

Sartre and Merleau-Ponty on the Communist Party

Right after the war, Maurice Merleau-Ponty joined Sartre, Simone de Beauvoir, and others in founding a Left-leaning journal of ideas and criticism called *Les Temps modernes* ('Modern Times', after Charlie Chaplin's film that Sartre so loved). It soon became the voice of French existentialism and continues to enjoy a wide circulation to this day. Its first issue (in the autumn of 1945) contained an introduction by Sartre that served as a kind of manifesto for the movement in its post-war period and offered a preview of the philosophical principles of the political engagement that would mark Sartre's public life. In particular, it stressed its commitment to the autonomy of the individual, to the defence of their rights, and to the need for solidarity in the pursuit of these goals. 'Totally committed and totally free, it is this free person who must be set free by expanding their possibilities of choice.' 'In sum', he explains the programme of their journal, 'our intention is to work toward producing certain changes in the Society that surrounds us'. The question was the nature of the 'solidarity' necessary to pursue these ends.

We have remarked on the rise and fall of Sartre's relations with the French Communist Party. Merleau-Ponty's was rather the inverse. Though he never joined the Party, he was sympathetic to Marxism and published *Humanism and Terror* (1947), which defended the violence necessary to establish and preserve a Communist State beset by enemies bent on its destruction. Curiously, these are the kinds of arguments that Sartre would later employ to the same end. By then, Merleau-Ponty had broken with Sartre and withdrawn from active political involvement. But in the first years of *Les Temps modernes*, they found themselves on the same page. Where Merleau-Ponty wrote in 1947 that 'political action is of its nature impure, because it is the action of one person upon another and because it is collective action', Sartre would produce a play entitled *Dirty Hands* arguing the same case the following year.

The occasion of their falling out was the Korean War. Merleau-Ponty read the Sino-Soviet intervention much as Sartre would later read the Russian intervention in Hungary and Czechoslovakia as examples of Soviet imperialism. Both men reacted against it but by a distance of 16 years. Though Merleau-Ponty was the editor in charge of the political desk at the journal, in his absence and knowing his view of the matter, Sartre published an essay critical of the American involvement in the Korean conflict. Merleau-Ponty resigned as editor-in-chief and went on to reject Soviet Marxism in *Adventures of the Dialectic* (1955), which included a scathing critique of Sartre's politics entitled 'Sartre and Ultrabolshevism'. To complete the tale, Simone de Beauvoir responded in kind the same

13. Maurice Merleau-Ponty reading his notes

Maurice Merleau-Ponty (1908–61)

Like Camus and Sartre, his father died while he was a child and he was raised by his mother. He was a classmate of Simone de Beauvoir's and two years behind Sartre at the *École Normale Supérieure*. His early studies were in empirical, especially Gestalt, psychology. His major work, the *Phenomenology of Perception*, appeared in 1945. He attended the University of Louvain, Belgium, to study Edmund Husserl's unpublished manuscripts, which figured importantly in his thought, as did the works of Heidegger subsequently. With Sartre, de Beauvoir, and others, he founded the avant-garde journal *Les Temps modernes*. He died abruptly at his desk at the age of 53.

year in an essay entitled 'Merleau-Ponty and Pseudo-Sartrism'. Another break was complete. The titles tell it all. Yet what might have been dismissed as a family feud, and Sartre's entourage was often referred to as 'the family', was actually a dramatization of the Cold War performed on the stage of French letters. The figures were opinion-makers and their differences rippled across the media. In terms of social consciousness, existentialism had come of age, and its growing pains were being registered in novels and plays as well as in the press.

Simone de Beauvoir and existential feminism

By the time she published her ground-breaking work *The Second Sex* (1949), Simone de Beauvoir was already famous. She had written several essays, including 'The Ethics of Ambiguity', a couple of novels, and a play, and was among the founders of *Les Temps modernes*. But this two-volume work was her major achievement. It remains perhaps the single most important philosophical text in what would subsequently be called the 'feminist' movement.

Simone de Beauvoir (1908–86)

Like Sartre, she was born and died in Paris. Like him as well, she attended the prestigious *École Normale Supérieure* from which most of France's leading intellectuals have graduated. She taught in high schools (*lycées*) around France but never in the university. One of the most famous women of the age, she was also one of the most public. Among her many plays, novels, philosophical treatises, and multi-volume memoirs, the work that consolidated her international reputation and served as a foundational text for the feminist movement was *The Second Sex* (1949). Though they never married, she and Sartre were partners most of their adult lives.

14. Simone de Beauvoir, always at work

The philosophical premise of the book is the existentialist thesis that human reality exists 'in-situation' and that this situation is fundamentally ambiguous and unstable. But we have seen that she anticipated Sartre in elaborating the social dimension of our situation. *The Second Sex* develops the concept of 'situation' by underscoring the role played by gender and its social construction. In its most famous phrase, she writes: 'One is not born a woman, one becomes one.' In effect, sex is not gender. The former is a biological fact, the latter a social construction. She devotes a large part of her study to the historical genesis of 'woman' and the secondary role assigned to the female in 'patriarchal' societies throughout history. Her basic question is 'How did woman became "Other" in the human race? How did hers become the "second" sex?'

Among the myths debunked is that of 'the eternal feminine', famously articulated by Goethe in his *Faust* but, in fact, the centuries-old concept of a timeless feminine essence that stands as the model of passivity and unapproachable purity in contrast with the implied masculine essence as one of activity and subjectivity. De Beauvoir argues that this holds women to an unrealistic standard and ignores the particularities of each woman's situation. In the existentialist sense, it is false because it is not sufficiently concrete. It does not resonate with the lived experience of individual women. Having agreed with Sartre in 'The Ethics of Ambiguity' that there is no human nature, she now insists that there is no essence of the feminine either, and for the same reason: existence precedes essence, it doesn't follow it. She takes this as an invitation to move from ontology to sociology and politics.

But the myth of the eternal feminine also places a burden on women because of its contradictory features. It presents woman as the mother and nurturer to whom we owe our lives and who deserves our loving gratitude but also as the source of our mortality (Eve in the Biblical Garden of Eden) and thus deserving of our hatred and blame. 'Woman sums up nature as Mother, Wife, and Idea; these forms now mingle and now conflict, and each of them wears a double visage'. De Beauvoir's point is that what is socially constructed can be socially (and politically) dismantled and the oppression of women that it fosters can thereby be relieved.

In what we now recognize as integral to the existentialist tradition, liberation of individuals is always possible. But in the socially conscious dimension of the movement, one realizes that we cannot act directly on the freedom of either the oppressors or the oppressed. Rather, our efforts must be aimed at changing what we observed Sartre calling 'the bases and structures of choice'. This is the meaning of de Beauvoir's text as a call to action. Not only does it raise our consciousness to a social problem, it describes the vehicles of the oppression and in this way suggests the means to begin rectifying these structures. Above all, her book is an attack on 'patriarchal' power structures and a call to raze them.

But as Sartre would later say of colonialism, though the meanness is in the system, one cannot exculpate individuals for simply acting 'like everyone else'. What might seem paradoxical, if not simply contradictory, becomes understandable once one recognizes the basic ambiguity of the human 'situation': the fact that it consists of the free transcendence of a conditioning structure. Again, we are faced with the contribution of each to the destruction or the continuance of the patriarchal system. Specifically, what de Beauvoir calls 'force of circumstance' in a book by that title is a real, though not decisive, influence, and this makes the appeal to individual effort problematic, as it is for many existentialists. For instance, 'how does one achieve gender-neutral language?' we would ask today. 'A word at a time' would be the vintage existentialist's answer. And yet this 'nominalist' approach ignores the force of circumstance, that is, the power of social causes such as public opinion and custom at work in language formation. Once Sartre and de Beauvoir discovered society, they had to come to terms with the phenomenon of properly social causality – a type of influence that enriches individual action, without dissolving it in some impersonal collective. One might describe this graphically as 'existentialism meets Marxism and tries to humanize it'. De Beauvoir was trying to do this in the case of women's liberation. This is a problem that Sartre will undertake to resolve more generally as he writes his *Critique of Dialectical Reason* in the following decade.

De Beauvoir concludes her lengthy study with the vision of the society, disalienated and free of oppression, that she hopes can be furthered by necessary socioeconomic changes but which also requires the cooperation of free agents among themselves:

> It is for man to establish the reign of liberty in the midst of the world of the given. To gain the supreme victory, it is necessary, for one thing, that by and through their natural differentiation men and women unequivocally affirm their brotherhood.

This view is quite similar to the ideal of *positive reciprocity* among free agents that Sartre gestures towards in his *Notebooks for an Ethics*, dating from the same time but not published until after his death, and which he calls 'fraternity' in the *Critique*.

Individuals in relation: social existentialism

It should be clear that existentialists are scarcely ivory-tower intellectuals. Long before Sartre spoke of 'commitment', Kierkegaard and Nietzsche were addressing the social ills of their time and, in Kierkegaard's case at least, could be found right in the thick of local polemics. With the subsequent upheavals caused by two world wars, so-called 'vintage' existentialists followed Zarathustra's advice and turned inevitable involvement into existential choice. 'Everyone has the war he deserves' and 'We were never so free as under the Occupation', as Sartre provocatively phrased it. Their 'choices' covered the spectrum: from Heidegger's unfortunate involvement in the world of politics to Camus's risking his life with the Resistance.

But if the movement came to recognize and allow for the 'force of circumstance', it did so in a manner that preserved a place for individual freedom and responsibility in the social field. In his *Search for a Method*, Sartre lays out the basic ontological claim: there are only individuals and real relations among them. In the *Critique*, he will go on to elaborate his understanding of how social groups and institutions can possess qualities that surpass their individual members without dissolving the latters' freedom and responsibility, which are enriched, in the case of group activity, or compromised, in the case of institutional inertia, but never completely destroyed.

Merleau-Ponty captured the realistic optimism of the existentialist position in the social arena when he extended Sartre's humanistic mantra to the social realm:

> The human world is an open or unfinished system and the same radical contingency which threatens it with discord also rescues it from the inevitability of disorder and prevents us from despairing of it, providing only that one remembers its various machineries are actually men and tries to maintain and expand man's relations to man.

Chapter 6
Existentialism in the 21st century

Remaining open to the adventures of experience.

Maurice Merleau-Ponty

Although 'existentialism' remains a frequently mentioned term and Sartre arguably the most widely recognized philosopher of the 20th century, one often hears the claim that the movement is over; that it has been supplanted by two successive waves of French thought, structuralism in the 1960s and poststructuralism in the 1970s and 1980s, after which the momentum dissipated as the cohort of philosophical personages passed away. Admittedly, as a phenomenon of popular Western culture, existentialism reached its high point in the years immediately following the end of the Second World War. This was the era of 'Apache' (ruffian) dancing, of jazz in smoke-filled Left-Bank clubs, of theatre of the absurd, and of freedom in almost every sense of the word. In its French expression, it was a child of the liberation. The intensity of that moment could scarcely have been maintained. And yet its spirit remained in the depths of Western society, to surface in various nonconformist movements of the following decades and perhaps flaming out in the events of May 1968.

Graffiti on Parisian walls during the student rebellion of 1968 proclaimed 'All power to the imagination' (*L'imagination au pouvoir*). This captures the spontaneity, the utopian hope, and, possibly, the ultimate futility of that student uprising, which has sometimes been described as the 'Sartrean' revolution. The remark epitomized the existentialist thesis that as beings in-situation we are creatures of the possible, of what Sartre called transcendence, or temporally speaking, the future. I have argued that for him 'transcendence' denotes primarily the activity of our imaging consciousness by which we reach beyond what we actually perceive to what could or might be perceived. No one has ever seen a unicorn but we have images of what one might see if such a creature existed in the physical world. As Sartre wrote in his study of novelist and playwright Jean Genet: 'The same insufficiency enables man to form images and prevents him from creating being.' Consciousness as the lack or insufficiency of being (as what he calls 'nothingness' in his title *Being and Nothingness*) depends on being the way our image of the unicorn depends on perceived horses, horns, and the like that consciousness cannot create but which it is free to fashion as it pleases. Our creative imagination is the expression of that freedom which defines us as human.

But Sartrean consciousness is committed; it is not simply free-floating reverie. And as the freedom that it pursues becomes increasingly concrete, that commitment grows more and more political, as does the 'imaginary' that expresses it. His ideal of the 'city of ends', where all relations are egalitarian (eye-level) and non-objectifying, constitutes the model to guide our social interchange. The relation between artist and public that Sartre characterizes as one of gift-appeal in which individuals communicate while respecting one another's freedom is now presented as the pattern for authentic social interaction in general. Not that Sartre is slipping into aestheticism (the substitution of the beautiful for the good, of art for morality). In fact, he writes of authentic love and friendship in similar terms in his posthumously published *Notebooks for an Ethics* – a view that will confound weekend existentialists who are accustomed to the analysis of (inauthentic) love portrayed in terms of sadism/masochism in *Being and Nothingness*.

As a cultural phenomenon, then, existentialism may have had its day. Yet even in a cultural sense, it has left its traces in the various subcultures that have succeeded it and in the vocabulary of anguish, bad faith, commitment, authenticity, and the like that continues to punctuate our discourse. Still, in this respect, it can be considered a period piece.

But as a philosophical movement, to the extent that it ever was one, existentialism in its various avatars has played a major role in Continental philosophy for over 50 years and has now entered the perennial philosophical conversation in which it voices the abiding moral concerns of the human condition. In other words, it continues to defend individual freedom, responsibility, and authenticity in the midst of various forms of determinism, conformism, self-deception, technologism, and the like so prevalent in our day. And it often does so in an imaginative mode that employs art and example to bring home in concrete fashion abstract principles that otherwise risk being dismissed as scholastic irrelevancies or admired from a distance as interesting intellectual curiosities. This is the kind of concrete philosophy that caused Sartre to 'blanche with emotion', in de Beauvoir's words, as their erstwhile friend Raymond Aron (1905–83) raised for them the possibility of giving a phenomenological description of the cocktail glass in front of them at a Parisian cafe in the early 1930s.

By way of example, let me discuss four areas of current philosophical debate, from several other likely candidates, to which the existentialists have already made or are poised to make significant contributions. While merely suggestive and scarcely full-blown elaborations, my reference to the following topics indicates the continued relevance of the authors presented in this volume to our contemporaries who seek to guide their lives in a truly human manner. What may be called the existentialist 'tradition' presents philosophy as a way of life and not a mere parlour game. In what follows we shall see how it promotes a return to experience from the 'linguistic turn' of Anglo-American philosophy without discounting the positive insights of the latter, a defence of human action against the dominance of abstract structural analyses while respecting the role of structures in our social relations, an elaboration of the richness of interpretation as fundamental to human existence as a complement to causal explanations in science and ordinary life, and a philosophy of responsibility that resonates with our concrete moral experience.

Experience and language

The 'linguistic turn' in Anglo-American philosophy away from experience, ideas, and systems of thought to the analysis of concepts and ordinary language is often seen as the move that separated so-called 'analytic' philosophers from their 'Continental' colleagues. In fact, existential philosophy took its own linguistic turn, inspired, on its French side, more by the posthumous publications of Swiss linguist Ferdinand de Saussure (1857–1913) than by Bertrand Russell (1872–1970) or Ludwig Wittgenstein (1889–1951). On its German side, this shift towards language was even more pronounced.

Consider the later Heidegger, for example. Though innocent of Saussurian linguistics, he spoke of language as the house of Being and accordingly employed 'philological' arguments to crack open our ordinary usages to reveal the Being that lay concealed therein. This was his practice even in his earlier, 'existentialist' writings. Consider his analysis of the word 'existence' (in German, *Exsistenz*) into the Latin 'ex' meaning 'out' as in 'exit' (goes out) and the verb 'sistere' (to stand), such that 'to exist' can be read as 'to stand out' from the crowd, from the average everyday, even (in Sartre's interpretation) from our very selves. Recall Sartre's claim that we are 'more' than ourselves, referring to our consciousness always moving beyond the present and actual to the future and possible. We have seen that when viewed temporally, *Exsistenz* denotes the future as not yet and as possibility. On this analysis, the term brings to our attention the temporal horizon on which traditionally timeless Being could now be understood. Some of Heidegger's 'parsings' of Classical Greek expressions often seemed forced and did not correspond with the common readings of Classical philologists. But they made perfectly good sense in the context of his attempted recovery of an original awareness of Being that, on his thesis, had been covered over and forgotten by the Western metaphysical tradition. The point in mentioning this approach is to emphasize that Heidegger assigned an importance to language which surpassed that of the philosophers of language in the English-speaking world. Nonetheless, he was not about to confuse the house with its inhabitant, however closely they might be related. Language may be the house of Being and we may be its guardians, but we are not its prisoners.

With Merleau-Ponty, this was also the case, especially in his early phenomenological approach to language. He sees language as expression and as one form of gesture among others, and he assigns to our lived bodies an intentionality that Husserl had reserved for consciousness. The concept of experience is thickened to entail the perspectives of our bodily existence. He insists that language ultimately is itself a form of existence. But with his discovery of the structural linguistics of Ferdinand de Saussure in the late 1940s, his understanding of language changes.

Before examining that change, let us pause to consider briefly the nature of a structuralist understanding of language and why it seems so contrary to an existentialist approach. At issue is the role of the free, responsible individual – the hallmark of existentialist thought. In brief, structuralism accords it little, if any, importance. As the name suggests, linguistic 'structuralism' studies the form or structure rather than the content of language. Like an X-ray technician before a body, the structuralist seeks to reveal the underlying organization of language rather than its 'flesh and blood' concrete employment. It considers language to be a systematic arrangement of signs that both make possible and limit communication, much like the skeleton both makes possible and limits how we can move. But unlike the skeleton in the X-ray, linguistic signs function in a 'differential' manner, that is, their 'meaning' depends on their difference from other signs within the same system or language (*langue*). In a real sense, one doesn't learn a word but a language. Without implicit reference to a natural language such as English or Swahili, the 'word' isn't even a word but a mere sound.

Linguistic signs, for the structuralist, do not 'name' objects as people commonly believe that words do, but rather differentiate among the members of a set of signs. The upshot is that meaning, for a structuralist, is a purely linguistic affair and not a relation between language and the world, as phenomenologists and the general public seem to think. This enables one to focus on the structures and codes of communication in a scientific way rather than get mired in the everyday ambiguities of individual conscious acts of speaking. But this drive towards the abstract and scientific leaves the existential, meaning-giving individual behind. In fact, structuralists discount the role of consciousness that forms the centre of existentialist philosophy and phenomenological method.

Under the influence of structuralist linguistics, Merleau-Ponty modifies his earlier consciousness-based understanding of language as expression in favour of a more formalist and differential approach employed by the structuralists. Language, he now claims, 'is the system of differentiations through which the individual articulates his relation to the world'. In other words, it is no longer the expression of meanings grasped intuitively by eidetic reduction, as Husserl maintained. Rather, it is a purely linguistic phenomenon, based on the comparative difference of signs among themselves in a system or 'language'.

But Merleau-Ponty remains sufficiently committed to the existentialist values of individual freedom and responsibility to resist total capitulation to the structuralist contention that the language 'speaks' us rather than the converse. What saves these values amidst structural forces is his distinction between being *determined* by socioeconomic factors (which he denies) and being *motivated* by the same (which he is willing to admit). His point is similar to that of so-called 'action theorists' in Anglo-American philosophy, who distinguish behaviour, which is caused and not free, from action for which reasons are given and where talk of freedom and responsibility is appropriate. Like Sartre, Merleau-Ponty is increasingly sensitive to the sociohistorical dimension of the meanings by which we interpret and guide our lives, whereas the structuralist approach tends to neglect the existential and historical in favour of ahistorical structures. He refers to this feature as the 'historicity of knowledge'. Sartre would later agree that we must learn to structure and categorize phenomena less rigidly. Merleau-Ponty is already reading phenomenological 'meanings' as historically contextualized. If not a capitulation to the relativism that Husserl eschewed, this view does suggest a certain nod towards pragmatism and the historical that maintains structure and practice, language and speech act in creative tension.

What sustains this tension is what Merleau-Ponty calls 'institution':

> What we understand by the concept of institution are those events in experience which endow it with durable dimensions, in relation to which a whole series of other experiences will acquire meaning, will form an intelligible series or a history – or again those events which sediment in me a meaning, not just as survivals and residues, but as the invitation to a sequel, the necessity of a future.

In other words, an institution is a set of events that 'structure' my experience but which experience, in turn, modifies and refashions. Rather than a closed set of all possible combinations such as Merleau-Ponty takes Saussure's 'language' or the kinship structures of Claude Lévi-Strauss' anthropology to be, institutions as structures are tables of 'diverse, complex probabilities, always bound to local circumstances' and thus open to 'the adventures of experience'. This is an existentialist adaptation of and contribution to structuralist accounts.

By his own admission, Sartre did not formulate a philosophy of language, but he insisted that the elements of one could be found throughout his works. Language, for him, was a phenomenon of expression that extended beyond words to nonverbal symbols and gestures. Like Merleau-Ponty, Sartre argues that the problem of language is exactly parallel to the problem of bodies: I cannot hear myself speak nor see myself smile.

Ontologically, language belongs to the category of 'being-for-others' in *Being and Nothingness* and to the domain of the 'practico-inert' in his *Critique of Dialectical Reason*. But in both cases, Sartre reads the move from language in general to natural languages such as French and German and then to dialects and slang, terminating in the individual speech act as a movement from the abstract to the increasingly concrete. The speech act of the situated individual would be the most concrete linguistic phenomenon. Language, on this account, is a basic technique for appropriating the world rather than the means of constituting it, as poststructuralists would insist. This exhibits Sartre's remark that 'freedom is the only possible foundation of the laws of language', a claim that structuralists would categorically deny. In other words, our freedom and responsibility extend to our choice of words and hence to the very language system (for example, the racist and sexist epithets) that we sustain by these choices. This is a typically existentialist understanding of language in its sensitivity to the implicit moral significance of our concrete acts of expression and communication. Yet it significantly limits the sense-making power of language as well as the claims of what has been called 'linguistic idealism', namely the denial that there is a reality external to and independent of language on which our use of words is supposed to be based.

But this abstract-concrete relation is historicized in Sartre's *Critique of Dialectical Reason* (1958). Now *praxis* (human activity in its sociohistorical context) has replaced being-for-itself or consciousness, and the *practico-inert* (the sedimented prior praxes that both limit and facilitate present praxes the way natural language limits and facilitates speech acts) has assumed the functions of being-in-itself or the nonconscious from *Being and Nothingness*. Unlike being-in-itself, the practico-inert is the site of counter-finality, the unintended consequences of our practical decisions. The practice of deforestation to increase arable land, for example, can produce the opposite effect by causing floods. Sartre cites this as a function of the *practico*-inert; that is, as an example of our prior praxes coming back to undermine our present projects. As before, the relation between language and the specific acts of speaking is one of abstract versus concrete. But the objective possibilities and the counter-finalities of language as practico-inert significantly refine the rather vague contrast of abstract/concrete in Sartre's earlier position. Great weight is now assigned to the power of language insofar as it exercises what structuralist Marxist Louis Althusser called a kind of 'structural causality' on our speech acts. With his concept of the practico-inert, Sartre, in fact, is recognizing the validity of Saussurian linguistics as Merleau-Ponty interpreted it, while continuing to insist on the existentialist primacy of individual praxis in his understanding of linguistic phenomena.

The upshot of this brief survey of existentialist approaches to language is to indicate the degree to which it is lived experience (in German, *Erlebnis*), or what Sartre calls *le vécu*, rather than language as such that constitutes the groundwork for their discussions. Language is important, but chiefly insofar as it expresses or fashions experience in a mutual but often strained relationship.

The threat of being confined in what Fredric Jameson called the 'prison-house of language' is scarcely a problem for the existentialists as it has been for many linguistic idealists both on the Continent and in the English-speaking world. Thanks to the Husserlian theory of intentionality, consciousness was always already 'in the world'. And even when their attention broadened from consciousness to lived experience, it was the experience of language and the language of experience rather than language as such that interested the existentialists. Though their early understanding of language was arguably instrumentalist, as exemplified by Sartre's unfortunate distinction in *What is Literature?* between poetry and prose in terms of their respective capacity for commitment, the writings of Merleau-Ponty were already moving beyond that somewhat oversimplified view towards a more structuralist conception of language at the time of his death. Sartre too would refine his earlier thesis to accommodate linguistic and other structures under the concept of the practico-inert in the *Critique*.

Structuralism and poststructuralism

I mentioned that the existentialist 'movement' was eclipsed by two successive schools of thought, namely structuralism and poststructuralism in that order, and their presence continues to be felt in our day. Whether they agreed to the identification or not, the leading members of the structuralist school of thought were popularly taken to be anthropologist Claude Lévi-Strauss, Marxist theorist Louis Althusser, psychoanalyst Jacques Lacan, literary critic and semiologist Roland Barthes, and, of course, structuralist linguist Ferdinand de Saussure, whose work in linguistics provided the theoretical basis for the movement as we saw in the previous section. Again, as the name suggests, structuralism is a somewhat Platonic approach to social phenomena that searches for the impersonal and necessary structures that unconsciously guide and limit our reasoning processes and practices. From that point of view, the reasoning processes of 'primitive' people are as logical as those of modern individuals. The method distinguishes the non-temporal considerations of a cultural practice such as the rules of language formation or the kinship regulations of a tribe from its developmental or historical aspects like the concrete way in which these rules are applied in practice. Structuralists pay more attention

113

to the non-temporal dimension of these phenomena in their quest for broad rules that will give their respective investigations general, scientific status. Thus kinship relations within a 'primitive' society, for example, can be shown to follow an unconscious 'logic' of largely binary relations (of inclusion and exclusion) that determine in advance who is permitted to marry whom and who is prohibited from doing so. In most Western legal systems, for instance, it is forbidden for individuals related as first cousins or closer to marry. But in so-called 'primitive' societies, as Lévi-Strauss demonstrated, that system of permitted and prohibited marriages follows far more complex rules than simply prohibition of consanguineous marriage. Ideally, such patterns or structures can be charted according to certain 'codes' that the structuralist scholar will decipher. In an analogous way, a similar unconscious logic can be observed operating in literary works (Barthes), in Marx's scientific socialism (Althusser), and in Lacan's famous decree that the unconscious is 'structured like a language' – a formulation that Sartre found quite attractive even as he continued to reject the concept of an unconscious.

Here too, what makes the structuralist antithetical to the existentialist approach to these topics is the impersonal, necessitating role assigned to these social structures; their claim to be objective and scientific. This marks the beginning of the

15. **Leading structuralists employing 'primitive' reason**

so-called 'decentring of the subject' that will become the explicit theme of poststructuralist thought. But what set this method in direct opposition to existential phenomenology and caused so much ink to spill was its avowed 'anti-humanism'. As Michel Foucault conjectured at the conclusion of his reputedly 'structuralist' masterpiece, *The Order of Things*, the success of structuralism in the 1960s suggests that an epistemic event may well occur in the near future that would change the fundamental structure of what we currently call 'knowledge' with an abruptness similar to the change that, he argued, brought our modern, man-centred mode of sense-making into being in the first place. If such a radical event were to occur, he surmised, 'one can certainly wager that man would be erased like a face drawn in the sand at the edge of the sea'. For these structures are no more the product of individual agency than were Plato's universal ideas or forms. Rather, individuals are the bearers and not the inventors of these structures in the same way they are the bearers not the inventors of the grammatical rules of the language they speak. The responsible individual on whom the existentialist concentrated is reduced to a 'place holder' in the impersonal structures of which he or she is usually ignorant.

This, of course, gives rise to the thorny problem of the meaning of agency and responsibility in a structuralist world. How can one be held responsible for the very social conditioning that has fashioned one into this kind of person? One observes here the recurrent problem of reconciling individual freedom and social science. To the extent that scientific laws and causes are necessitating, they leave no room for freedom in the existentialist sense. But the structuralists claimed to be on the trail of just such a 'scientific' approach to social phenomena that was modelled on if not grounded in the 'logic' of language itself.

We have observed how Merleau-Ponty was in the process of reconciling existentialist values of freedom and responsibility with scientific methods of structural linguistics, and potentially with the several structuralist applications of this method to what the

French call the human sciences (*Les sciences humaines*). Sartre, in *Search for a Method*, which served as an introduction to his *Critique of Dialectical Reason*, insisted that the task of existentialism was to 'reconquer man within Marxism'. What he had in mind was to defeat the Marxist 'economism' (economic determinism) of the party hacks; but his critique would prove equally relevant to the more sophisticated structuralist Marxism of Althusser and his followers that would gain prominence in the mid-1960s. In his *Critique*, as just mentioned, Sartre reserves an ontological place for structure and structuralist studies in the domain of the 'practico-inert' and the analytic reasoning that it supports. Again, Althusser's 'structural causes' can be located in the practico-inert domain, as can Lévi-Strauss' kinship trees. This is a major function of the concept of the practico-inert that is often overlooked. But as we said earlier, as *practico*-inert, the concept guards individual freedom and responsibility even in relation to our most impersonal and 'necessary' social structures. For example, Sartre raises the question of how these kinship structures of Lévi-Strauss operate in time of population scarcity due to war or natural disaster. His implication is that they do not, that we do not serve the structures, they serve us. Merleau-Ponty's interpretation of structures as 'probabilities' rather than as 'necessities' preserves existential freedom as well. Again the humanist motto: 'You can always make something out of what you've been made into.'

What has come to be known as 'poststructuralism' in philosophy or 'postmodernism' in literature, art, and architecture is characterized by what Jean-François Lyotard (in whom these categories overlap) calls the 'fission of meaning'. Just as nuclear fission (splitting or break-up) emits large amounts of energy, so the break-up of the standard unities of genre and narrative, of form and style, of organic relation and hierarchical ordering, and, above all, of substance and self, have yielded multiplicities and interspersions. Similarly, the structuralist binary oppositions that revealed the 'logic' of social and cultural relations are broken up by poststructuralists like Foucault into a plurality of rationalities. While Kierkegaard and Nietzsche are reinstated as anti-modernist thinkers because of their multiple concepts of truth and their respective emphases on the power of willing and the will to power, Sartrean existentialism is dismissed as incurably modernist because of its alleged reliance on the Cartesian *Cogito* as the starting point of philosophical reasoning. Foucault can be taken as representing the poststructuralist movement when he remarks in a particularly severe dismissal: *'The Critique of Dialectical Reason* is the magnificent and pathetic attempt by a man of the nineteenth century to think the twentieth century. In that sense, Sartre is the last Hegelian and, I would say, the last Marxist.' In other words, in Foucault's opinion, Sartrean existentialism has nothing to say to the contemporary mind.

Notwithstanding the reckless vehemence of Foucault's critique, it is impossible to confine Sartre even to the century that he doubtless emblematized for at least two reasons. The Sartrean subject, as I pointed out, is not a self but a presence-to-self. We have seen that it is precisely *non*-self-identical, which invites fruitful dialogue with postmodern and/or poststructuralist authors like Barthes and Foucault who speak of the 'death' of the author and the 'eclipse' of the self. Though a fundamental dualism does pervade Sartre's thought, it is not the commonly rejected duality of mind and body, of thinking and extended substances *à la* Descartes, but a dualism of spontaneity and inertia – a functional, not substantial, duality that is compatible with poststructuralist thought.

Secondly, though Sartre does not subscribe to a multiplicity of rationalities, he has clearly distinguished two such in his *Critique*, namely dialectical and analytical reason. The former is dynamic and historical, the latter is neither. This raises the possibility of other forms of reasoning besides these two. Moreover, he has linked each of them with a political and social class, the proletariat and the bourgeoisie respectively, in a bow towards the Foucauldian (and Nietzschean) unity of knowledge and power – a postmodernist thesis. In fact, Sartre's claim that 'all knowledge is committed' not only expresses his concept of life-orienting Choice but also introduces the power-knowledge issue in a somewhat Nietzschean sense well before Foucault made that relationship prominent once more. And if Sartre is suspicious of the Freudian unconscious for its threat to individual freedom, he is equally critical of the sceptical perspectivism and multiple rationalities that he believes discourage radical social change and thereby favour the socioeconomic status quo. This was already his criticism of his former friend Raymond Aron's approach to historical understanding in the late 1930s.

When one adds de Beauvoir's continued, if sometimes disputed, presence in the current feminist movement, one can conclude that, without being postmodernists *avant la lettre*, both she and Sartre can join the proto-existentialists, Kierkegaard and Nietzsche, in also furthering this aspect of the philosophical conversation in the 21st century.

Hermeneutics

The increased importance of philosophical hermeneutics in the 20th century also contributed a momentum to carry existentialist thought into the 21st. As the method of interpreting a text, originally a Biblical and then a legal and finally any literary or artistic text, hermeneutics has played an important role in Continental thought. As the notion of 'text' came to include the manifestation of any intentional act from the founding of an institution to the jabs and feints of a boxer, the scope of hermeneutical interpretation expanded accordingly. With Wilhelm Dilthey (1833–1911) and Max Weber (1864–1920), the use of 'understanding' became the defining method of the human sciences, especially history and humanistic sociology (*Verstehende Soziologie*) as distinct from the natural sciences. At the hands of Heidegger and especially his student Hans-Georg Gadamer (1900–2002) 'understanding' and interpretation became our fundamental manner of being-in-the-world.

Like phenomenology, hermeneutics is primarily a method and not a metaphysical or ontological theory. It assumes that all knowledge is contextual ('situated', as Sartre would say) and that the knower comes to a problem with a 'prejudice' or pre-understanding of the issue at hand. This is an ancient problem, as old as the sophistical argument that learning is impossible because either you knew it already and hence cannot learn it or it is so foreign to you that you would not recognize it if ever you encountered it. Hermeneutics insists that learning is indeed possible because we both know and do not know whatever we are learning. The problem is to explain in which sense this paradoxical claim holds true. This is commonly called the 'hermeneutic circle'. Gadamer, the best-known practitioner of hermeneutics in our day, defines it as '[letting] what is alienated by the character of the written word or by the character of being distantiated by cultural or historical research speak again'. In other words, it is a method for discerning the meaning of an unfamiliar text, whether its strangeness be historical, like an ancient inscription, or simply foreign to us, like the statements of someone from another culture or even from another profession or academic speciality. It was introduced into modern philosophy by Friedrich Schleiermacher (1768–1834) and extended to the human sciences by Dilthey and Weber. Taken in the broad sense of 'comprehending' another's action as opposed to 'explaining' it causally (which might jeopardize one's freedom), the existentialists employed it extensively, each in his or her own way. A brief review of five of our figures will reveal its use at their hands as well as how 'existential' hermeneutics bears continued relevance to current discussions of the topic.

The first was Nietzsche, no admirer of Schleiermacher, who insisted that all knowledge was interpretation and denied that there was any fundamental 'text' beyond which one could no longer move in an attempt to comprehend it definitively. Knowledge could never be absolute or apodictic; it was interpretation of interpretation all the way down. This seems to lead to a kind of pragmatist approach to truth and knowledge that both Nietzsche and the postmodernists favour. On this account, knowledge is like treading water and truth is our success in doing so. This is a far cry from Husserl's phenomenology, which was intended to combat just such 'relativism' as well as the 'voluntarism' (emphasis on will over intellect in relating to the world) that he believed it fostered.

The anti-Cartesian nature of hermeneutical method comes to the fore with Martin Heidegger. We are now in the midst of the hermeneutical circle just mentioned. Heidegger argues that one already has an inkling (what he calls a 'pre-understanding') of the subject one is investigating prior to its actual pursuit, otherwise one would not be interested at all. It was Heidegger who rendered phenomenology hermeneutical. In fact, his masterwork, *Being and Time*, is one extended effort to articulate our pre-understanding of Being that makes our own existence problematic to us. It is also one reason why his mentor, Husserl, refused to recognize Heidegger's as authentic phenomenology.

Sartre continues this line of inquiry in *Being and Nothingness* where he appeals to our 'preontological comprehension' of an array of interrelated topics from being and non-being to the criteria of truth and one's fundamental project. The task of phenomenological description is to bring this implicit awareness to reflective consciousness. Such comprehension is immediate and precognitive. It affords a concrete guide for our subsequent investigations that are mediated by reflection and articulated in concepts.

Karl Jaspers adopted the Diltheyan and Weberian method of applying hermeneutics to the human sciences, particularly to psychology and history. The concept of comprehension (*Verstehen*) that Dilthey formulated and which Weber employed with such effect was introduced in France by Raymond Aron in the late 1930s. In fact, it was Aron's work that sparked Sartre's interest in the philosophy of history. Jaspers and the others shared the Diltheyan ideal of a textual hermeneutic that would enable one 'to understand an author better than he understood himself'. An important instrument in Jaspers's psychopathology, as it would later be in

Sartre's existential psychoanalysis, hermeneutics served to 'humanize' the human sciences by giving us access to their 'inner life'; that is, to the intentions and purposes that move agents to action as distinguished from the natural 'causes' that explain their behaviour.

But Sartre introduces a particularly existentialist-humanist use of hermeneutics towards the end of *Being and Nothingness* when he adopts it as the method of 'existential psychoanalysis'. The aim of this project is to bring to reflective consciousness the basic 'Choice', or life-defining project, of an individual. As we noted in Chapter 4, it assumes that a life is a totalizing phenomenon like the progression of a narrative, the unity of which depends on a pre-reflective and sustained adoption of a set of values and criteria that give meaning/direction (*sens*) to that life. Since pre-consciousness is completely translucent and implicitly self-aware, the task of the existential analyst, who can be the subject him- or herself, is to bring this comprehension to full knowledge. This is achieved with the help of a hermeneutic or interpretation of the empirical signs of the basic Choice. Like someone walking along a sandy beach, one can 'read' one's direction by looking back at one's footprints. Existential psychoanalysis seeks to reveal, not who, in bad faith, we pretend to be or erroneously think we are, but who our previous actions reveal we have Chosen (capital 'C') to be. Though he does not use the expression formulated by hermeneuticist Gadamer, Sartre seems to require a kind of 'fusion' of interpretive horizons between the analyst and the analysand to bring this off. But he does speak of our 'comprehension of another's comprehension' in ordinary social experiences as well as in writing an existential biography such as that of Gustave Flaubert. This would seem to be the functional equivalent of the fusion of horizons in the successful act of interpretation.

Moreover, the hermeneutic method assumes that a linguistic expression or any cultural object is embedded in a tradition. But this tradition can either impede communication or foster it, depending on the proper hermeneutical method employed. Although Dilthey defended hermeneutics as the proper method of the human sciences (*Geisteswissenschaften*) as distinct from the method of functional relations and causal explanations employed by the natural sciences (*Naturwissenschaften*), Heidegger describes 'understanding' as the human's fundamental way of being-in-the-world. It follows that the method of understanding (*Verstehen*) is not simply a complement to the natural sciences, as Dilthey seemed to imply and as Weber urged, but is the basis of human knowing in general. Sartre would seem to agree with Heidegger in that our pre-reflective awareness in *Being and Nothingness* is elaborated as 'comprehension' in the *Critique*, where it is described as simply the translucidity of praxis to itself. Hermeneutics would then be a universal method, appropriate to all forms of human understanding. And yet Sartre, who links hermeneutics with dialectical reason and praxis, wishes to retain a place for 'analytical' reason as employed in the natural sciences. And to this extent he agrees with Dilthey and Weber. But he clouds this translucidity when he introduces the notion of 'ideology', or false consciousness, into the mix. This need not concern us here, except to warn us that the unblinking eye of Sartrean consciousness is more liable to visual complications than was previously recognized. Yet even if this qualifies the scope of human freedom and responsibility, it scarcely removes it.

An ethics of responsibility

In a post-postmodernist world, the inherited fragmentation of unifying principles and absolute values constitutes a particular challenge to ethical theory and moral practice in any recognizable sense of those terms. To start with, the very notion of an ethical identity seems to assume what Dilthey called 'the connectedness of a life'. From Ancient times, moralists have insisted on consistency as an essential ingredient in a moral life. Authentic existence in the Heideggerian sense entails the overcoming of the 'dissipation' of our efforts in sheer busyness and idle curiosity. Both he and Sartre look towards a resolute and sustaining project or 'Choice' to achieve this unity rather than taking refuge in some form of substantial identity. Each philosopher conceives of the human being as a responsible individual. And while Heidegger was reluctant to venture an ethics until the ontological question of the meaning of Being had been fully addressed (which never happened), Sartre was eager to 'give the bourgeoisie a guilty conscience' by drawing attention to those pockets of bad faith (such as denials of responsibility) that punctuate our everyday lives. For Sartre, responsibility, like freedom, is everywhere.

The popularity of French ethicist Emmanuel Levinas (1905–95) in postmodern ethics opens a door to the revival of existentialist concepts and values, though he was not commonly viewed as an existentialist. What attracted many postmodern thinkers to Levinas's position was its rejection of a metaphysical foundation for ethics and its turn to an ethics of responsibility in place of one of universal principles or abstract values. If Levinas had not existed, the postmodernists would have had to invent him.

Yet even postmodernists acknowledged the need for basic ethical principles such as 'justice', which Jacques Derrida famously claimed was 'perhaps undeconstructable'. By this, he meant that it was perhaps not liable to Derrida's usual method (deconstruction) of unravelling the unity of a concept by analysis of the 'loose ends' or 'traces' that it harboured from a prior metaphysical assumption. More simply put, justice was perhaps an absolute in a relativistic world.

Levinas likewise accorded justice a certain relative ultimacy. For Levinas, justice is derived from the advent of the third party even though it is based on the original responsibility of the face-to-face, his fundamental ethical category. In this sense, justice resembles Sartre's concept of the upsurge of our 'being-for-others' with the appearance of a third person in our midst. As with the utilitarians before them, the postmodernists have found the concept of justice their Achilles' heel. It seems to bear a non-negotiable character to which they must comply. No amount of 'gaming' (as Lyotard proposed by considering justice an especially serious game) or metaphorical sleight of hand succeeds in escaping its stark demands. And yet, as with Kierkegaard's tragic hero, impersonal justice, indifferent to 'attenuating circumstances', can cause great harm.

It is at this point that the existentialists' concept of being-in-situation offers help. Again, it is a case of sensitivity to concrete thinking. And once more, it is not so much a matter of introducing novel ideas as of calling us back to insights that are traditional even if their conceptual context is not. Two such appeals to 'concrete' thinking in Aristotle come to mind, namely his distinction between justice and fairness (equity) and his concept of the prudent person. In the former instance, one can avoid the unfairness of the acontextual application of the law by considering the particularities of the case. The distinction between the letter and the spirit of the law is another expression of this same attention to the concrete.

In a sense, the notion of an ethic of situations is not news. It is at least as ancient as Aristotle's concept of the prudent person (*phronimos*), our second example. This is the one who knows the right thing to do at the right time in the right circumstance. Prudence, as ethicist Josef Pieper says, may be understood as 'situation conscience'. There is an obvious concreteness about 'prudential' judgements in the Aristotelian sense. They are the fruit of a certain non-vicious circularity: the virtuous person is someone who makes virtuous judgements, but one must learn to be a virtuous person by making such judgements. That's just the way it is. There is no absolute starting point. One is always *in medias res*. We find ourselves in the ethical version of the hermeneutic circle.

Like the prudent person, the existentialist judges 'in-situation'. But where the prudent person *discovers* what is the right thing to do, the existentialist *decides* what is the right thing to do. He or she is 'creative' where the Aristotelian is investigatory. The 'authentic' individual decides in full recognition of the fallibility of his or her judgement. But having made the choice in view of the best available evidence, not just arbitrarily, and in view of the promotion of freedom, the authentic person, as we saw, will make it the right choice by their follow-through.

It is into this field of ethical free-fall that the existentialist meets the postmodernists' demands for an ethical practice without metaphysical commitment or inviolable laws and principles. As we have suggested, the Sartrean view of an ethic of value-appropriation that expresses and sustains freedom throughout a person's life can begin to meet these postmodernist requirements in a post-postmodern world. If the modernist view of ethics, as ethicist Zygmunt Bauman claims, is to insist that the conflict between the autonomy of rational animals and the heteronomy of rational management (between ends and means), though not yet resolved, is resolvable in principle, while the postmodern position consists in the willing endorsement of this non-resolvability and a fostering of the multiplicity of options that this allows, the existentialist stand offers post-postmodernism both the power of an ethical ideal (for example, authentic existence in Sartre's city of ends) and the clear-eyed willingness to live with inevitable ambiguity, as Merleau-Ponty and de Beauvoir propose. This is not far from the Aristotelian warning not to seek greater precision in the moral realm than it allows and, specifically, not to look for quantitative solutions to moral problems. And if the existentialist option meets the postmodern requirement of being unmetaphysical, and so in this respect is decidedly non-Aristotelian, it remains 'modernist' in its commitment to a humanism but to one of its own fashioning.

References

Chapter 1

Albert Camus, *The Plague* (New York: Vintage, 1991)

Pierre Hadot and Arnold Davidson, *Philosophy as a Way of Life: Spiritual Exercises from Socrates to Foucault* (Oxford: Blackwell, 1995)

Søren Kierkegaard, *Concluding Unscientific Postscript to Philosophical Fragments*, tr. Howard V. Hong and Edna H. Hong (Princeton, NJ: Princeton University Press, 1992)

—— *Papers and Journals: A Selection* (London: Penguin Books, 1996)

Dermot Moran, *Introduction to Phenomenology* (London: Routledge, 2000)

Jean-Paul Sartre, 'Intentionality: A Fundamental Idea of Husserl's Phenomenology', *Journal of the British Society for Phenomenology*, 1 (2): 5

—— *Sketch for a Theory of the Emotions* (London: Routledge, 2002)

—— *What is Literature? And Other Essays* (Cambridge, MA: Harvard University Press, 1998)

Chapter 2

Joakim Garff, *Søren Kierkegaard: A Biography* (Princeton, NJ: Princeton University Press, 2005)

Karl Jaspers, *Basic Philosophical Writings* (Atlantic Highlands, NJ: Humanities Press, 1994)

Søren Kierkegaard, *Either/Or*, 2 vols., tr. Howard V. Hong and Edna H. Hong (Princeton, NJ: Princeton University Press, 1987); an abridged version in one volume, tr. Alastair Hannay (London: Penguin, 1992)

—— *Fear and Trembling* and *Repetition*, tr. Howard V. Hong and Edna H. Hong (Princeton, NJ: Princeton University Press, 1983)

—— *Stages on Life's Way*, tr. Howard V. Hong and Edna H. Hong (Princeton, NJ: Princeton University Press, 1988)

Friedrich Nietzsche, *The Anti-Christ, Ecce Homo, Twilight of the Idols: And Other Writings* (Cambridge: Cambridge University Press, 2005)

—— *Beyond Good and Evil* (Cambridge: Cambridge University Press, 2001)

Jean-Paul Sartre, 'Existentialism is a Humanism', in Walter Kaufmann (ed.), *Existentialism: From Dostoevsky to Sartre* (London: Penguin Plume, 1988)

Chapter 3

Saul Bellow, *Herzog* (New York: Viking, 1961)

Albert Camus, *The Myth of Sisyphus and Other Essays* (New York: Vintage, 1991)

Gabriel Marcel, *The Philosophy of Existentialism* (New York: Citadel, 1961)

Maurice Merleau-Ponty, 'The Battle over Existentialism', *Sense and Non-Sense* (Evanston, IL: Northwestern University Press, 1964)

Friedrich Nietzsche, *Human, All Too Human: A Book for Free Spirits* (Cambridge: Cambridge University Press, 1986)

—— *Thus Spoke Zarathustra* (New York: Viking Compass, 1966)

Jean-Paul Sartre, *Being and Nothingness* (New York: Citadel, 1984)

—— *Nausea* (New York: New Directions, 1969)

Chapter 4

Simone de Beauvoir, *The Ethics of Ambiguity* (New York: Citadel, 2000)

Jean-Paul Sartre, *Being and Nothingness* (New York: Citadel, 1984)

—— *Notebooks for an Ethics* (Chicago: University of Chicago Press, 1992), pp. 474–515

Leo Tolstoy, *The Death of Ivan Ilyich* (New York: Bantam Books, 2004)

Chapter 5

Simone de Beauvoir, *The Second Sex* (New York: Knopf, 1989)

Karl Jaspers, *The Future of Mankind* (Chicago: University of Chicago Press, 1968)

—— *The Question of German Guilt* (Bronx, NY: Fordham University Press, 2001)

Søren Kierkegaard, *Two Ages: The Age of Revolution and the Present Age. A Literary Review* (Princeton, NJ: Princeton University Press, 1978)

Gabriel Marcel, *Man Against Mass Society* (Chicago: Gateway, 1970)

Maurice Merleau-Ponty, *Humanism and Terror: The Communist Problem* (Somerset, NJ: Transaction Publishers, 2000)

Rüdiger Safranski, *Martin Heidegger: Between Good and Evil* (Cambridge, MA: Harvard University Press, 1998)

Jean-Paul Sartre, *The Condemned of Altona* (New York: Vintage, 1963)

Chapter 6

Zygmunt Bauman, *Postmodern Ethics* (Oxford: Blackwell, 1993)

Catherine Belsey, *Poststructuralism: A Very Short Introduction* (Oxford: Oxford University Press, 2002)

Jean Grondin, *Introduction to Philosophical Hermeneutics* (New Haven, CT: Yale University Press, 1994)

Martin Heidegger, 'Letter on Humanism', *Martin Heidegger: Basic Writings*, ed. David Krell (San Francisco: Harper, 1993)

Jean-Paul Sartre, *Critique of Dialectical Reason*, vol. 1 (London: Verso, 2002) and vol. 2 (London: Verso, 2006)

John Sturrock, *Structuralism*, 2nd edn. (Oxford: Blackwell, 2003)

Further reading

General introductions and surveys

An older but still valuable introduction to existentialism is *Irrational Man: A Study in Existential Philosophy* by William Barrett (New York: Anchor Books, 1962, 2nd edn. 1990). Two helpful collections of writings by leading existentialist authors are *Existentialism: Basic Writings*, ed. Charles Guignon and Derk Pereboom (Indianapolis, IN: Hackett, 1995) and *The Existentialist Reader: An Anthology of Key Texts*, ed. Paul S. MacDonald (New York: Routledge, 2001). Someone wishing to pursue essays on the basic concepts of existential and phenomenological thought by a variety of authors, as well as existential and phenomenological contributions to a number of topics in current philosophical discussion should consult Hubert L. Dreyfus and Mark A. Wrathall (eds.), *A Companion to Existentialism and Phenomenology* (Oxford: Blackwell, 2006).

Chapter-length essays on existentialism, phenomenology, and most of the individual philosophers discussed here, along with helpful suggestions for further reading, are available in the *Stanford Encyclopedia of Philosophy*, online at *http://plato.stanford.edu*. Relevant essays on individual philosophers can be found in *The Macmillan Encyclopedia of Philosophy*, 2nd edn. (Farmington Hills, MI: Thomson Gale, 2006); *The Routledge History of Philosophy*, especially vol. 7, *The Nineteenth Century*, ed. C. L. Ten, and vol. 8, *Continental Philosophy in the 20th Century*, ed. Richard Kearney

(London: Routledge, 1994); *The Edinburgh Encyclopedia of Continental Philosophy*, ed. Simon Glendinning (Edinburgh: Edinburgh University Press, 1999); and *A Companion to Continental Philosophy*, ed. Simon Critchley and William Schroeder (Oxford: Blackwell, 1998).

Philosophy as a way of life

Those interested in this topic might consult Pierre Hadot, *What is Ancient Philosophy?* (Cambridge, MA: Harvard University Press, 2004), Michel Foucault, *Fearless Speech* (Los Angeles, CA: Semiotext(e), 2004), and Alexander Nehamas, *The Art of Living: Socratic Reflections from Plato to Foucault* (Berkeley: University of California Press, 1998). Among the many arresting examples of the overlap between existential philosophy and imaginative literature are Fyodor Dostoevsky's *Notes from Underground* (New York: Penguin, 2004) and Franz Kafka's *The Trial* (New York: Schocken Books, 1998), or its film version by Orson Welles (1963) with Anthony Perkins (DVD). A concise introduction to the thought of Husserl is Robert Sokolowski's *Introduction to Phenomenology* (Cambridge: Cambridge University Press, 1999).

Becoming an individual

A valuable survey of this topic is *Becoming a Self: A Reading of Kierkegaard's Concluding Unscientific Postscript*, by Merold Westphal (West Lafayette, IN: Purdue University Press, 1996). Individualizing choice is a theme of Sartre's play *The Flies* in *No Exit and Three Other Plays* (New York: Vintage, 1989). Albert Camus's *The Outsider* (London: Penguin, 1970), translated in America as *The Stranger*, is a classic study of becoming an existentialist individual. Of the many existential themes not treated here, 'alienation' is certainly a major one. To fill this gap, consider Richard Schmitt's *Alienation and Freedom* (Boulder, CO: Westview Press, 2003). An excellent biography of Nietzsche is provided by Rüdiger Safranski, *Nietzsche: A Philosophical Biography* (New York: Norton, 2002).

Humanism: for and against

A helpful historical survey is Tony Davies's *Humanism* (London: Routledge, 1997). For an introduction to atheistic or naturalist humanism, consider Richard Norman's *On Humanism* (London: Routledge, 2004). For a theistic critique, see Henri de Lubac, *The Drama of Atheistic Humanism* (San Francisco: Ignatius Press, 1995). Two relevant classics are Martin Buber's *I and Thou* (New York: Touchstone, 1996) and Paul Tillich's *The Courage to Be* (New Haven, CT: Yale University Press, 2000).

Authenticity

A valuable overview is Jacob Golomb's *In Search of Authenticity: From Kierkegaard to Camus* (London: Routledge, 1995). *The Ethics of Authenticity* by Charles Taylor (Cambridge, MA: Harvard University Press, 1991) has rightly become an influential study of this topic by a non-existentialist. Charles Guignon's *On Being Authentic* (London: Routledge, 2004) assesses the strengths and weaknesses of this concept in an accessible manner. Two careful studies of this topic in Sartre's thought are Ronald E. Santoni's *Bad Faith, Good Faith, and Authenticity in Sartre's Early Philosophy* (Philadelphia: Temple University Press, 1995) and Joseph S. Catalano's *Good Faith and Other Essays: Perspectives on Sartre's Ethics* (Lanham, MD: Rowman and Littlefield, 1996).

Existentialism and social thought

De Beauvoir's autobiography, especially *Force of Circumstance*, covering 1944–62 (New York: Putnam, 1965), and *All Said and Done*, covering 1962–72 (New York: Putnam, 1974), provides a first-hand account of those years of the existentialist movement. William McBride, *Sartre's Political Theory* (Bloomington, IN: Indiana University Press, 1991) offers a thorough analysis of Sartre's political thought throughout his life. Thomas R. Flynn, *Sartre and Marxist Existentialism: The Test Case of Collective Responsibility* (Chicago: University of Chicago Press, 1984) analyses Sartre's social ontology. Many of Merleau-Ponty's political essays are reprinted in *Sense and Non-Sense* and in *Signs* (Evanston, IL: Northwestern University Press, 1964, both texts). Daniel Conway argues for the political significance of Nietzsche's thought in *Nietzsche and the Political* (New York: Routledge, 1996). Similarly, see Tracy B. Strong, *Friedrich Nietzsche and the Politics of Transfiguration* (Urbana, IL: University of Illinois Press, 2000).

Existentialism in the 21st century

A rich and useful study is *Kierkegaard in Post/Modernity*, ed. Martin J. Matuštík and Merold Westphal (Bloomington, IN: Indiana University Press, 1995). *The Cambridge Companion to Nietzsche*, ed. Bernd Magnus and Kathleen Higgins (Cambridge: Cambridge University Press, 1996) contains several relevant essays. The collection *Questioning Ethics: Contemporary Debates in Continental Philosophy*, ed. Richard Kearney and Mark Dooley (London: Routledge, 1999) brings existentialist concepts and authors into the recent discussion either explicitly or by implication. Gary Gutting, *Foucault: A Very Short Introduction* (Oxford: Oxford University Press, 2005) introduces Sartre into the discussion, as does Thomas R. Flynn, *Sartre, Foucault and Historical Reason*, 2 vols (Chicago: University of Chicago Press, 1997 and 2005).

Glossary

anguish (*Angst, l'angoisse*): Awareness of one's freedom as radical possibility. This differs from 'fear', which has a specific object. Thus one might fear falling off a cliff but feel anguish before the possibility of throwing oneself over.

authenticity: The state of acknowledging one's distinctive individuality. For Heidegger, this involves resolutely embracing one's being-unto-death; for Sartre, it is owning one's radical freedom and responsibility. Each existentialist has his or her version of this 'virtue'.

communication, indirect: The oblique way of gaining the sympathetic attention of the audience in order to convey values and feelings that otherwise might be intellectualized or simply rejected out of hand. The fine arts are particularly effective at this form of 'concrete' thinking.

Dasein: Heidegger's term for the properly human way of being. By using this term rather than 'man', he avoids the traditional *humanism* that unwittingly limits a human's distinctiveness by focusing on the claim that man is a 'rational animal'.

existence: Etymologically, it means to 'stand out'. Humans exist; things simply are. The existentialists link it with *temporality*, *ekstatic* especially with the future as possibility. It is best captured by similes such as Kierkegaard's: 'What does it mean to exist? To exist is to stand in a very long line and then not buy a ticket when you reach the window. No, to exist is to be desperately grasping the mane of a horse as it races across the plane. No, to exist is like being in the greatest possible hurry as you ride on the back of a poky pony.' (See *communication, indirect*.)

faith, bad: Sartre's term for the self-deception to which everyone is liable by virtue of the bivalent composition of the human *situation*, namely its facticity and transcendence. *Authentic* existence maintains this duality in a creative tension. Bad faith attempts to flee the tension (and its *anguish*) by either collapsing the transcendence into facticity or volatilizing the facticity into transcendence. Both attempts are a denial of our ontological make-up and for that reason futile.

hermeneutics: The method of interpreting or understanding the meaning of 'texts', taken broadly to include dreams, symbols, and the intentions of other agents, including oneself.

humanism: The philosophical theory that places the human at the centre of the universe. Its forms – for example atheistic, religious, Marxist, Renaissance, Classical Greek, and the like – depend on what they take to be the greatest perfection attainable by a human being.

intentionality: The defining characteristic of consciousness for Husserl, whereby it aims at (intends) an object in the world. This frees the phenomenologist from the problem of the 'bridge' between mind and external reality bequeathed modern philosophy by the 'inside/outside' epistemology of René Descartes (1596–1650).

nihilism: The belief that there are no objective values, that truth is purely subjective, and that human existence is meaningless. Nietzsche believed that the 'herd' would succumb to a certain kind of nihilism following its loss of faith in God, but that 'free spirits' would survive this plague by embracing this situation and creating their own truths and values.

phenomenology: One of the leading philosophical movements of the 20th century, it was founded by Edmund Husserl. As a method of rigorously describing the objects of consciousness, it was employed by existentialists like Heidegger and Sartre.

postmodernism: More of a critical alternative to than a successor of modernism, it rejects the emphasis on the subject and on consciousness that characterizes both *phenomenology* and existentialism. Though the term has come to be used so broadly as to be practically meaningless, in the words of its leading proponent, Jean-François Lyotard (1924–98), it refuses 'master narratives' such as the Marxist theory of history as class struggle and proclaims the 'fission' of meaning, that is, the irreparable break-up of unified sense-making in contemporary society.

poststructuralism: Often conflated with postmodernism, this is more philosophical and social-scientific in character than the more literary and aesthetic postmodernism. It too moves beyond the 'formalism' of structuralism in favour of a multiplicity of rationalities and a critique of the meaning-giving subject of *phenomenology* and existentialism. The movement would include Michel Foucault (1926–84) and other former structuralists, such as Jacques Lacan (1901–81) and Roland Barthes (1915–80), among its number.

situation: Humans exist 'in-situation', meaning that they are immersed in the givens of their conscious lives such as their parentage, nationality, gender, social identity, and previous choices. This is their 'facticity'. But they also 'transcend' those givens by the manner in which they relate to their facticity; for example, with shame or pride, with resignation or refusal, in hope or despair. The human situation is an inherently ambiguous mixture of these two components, facticity and transcendence, the given and the taken. (See *faith, bad*.)

structuralism: As the term suggests, it is the theory that our social interactions, beginning with our language (Ferdinand de Saussure) but extending to the logic of 'primitive' societies (Claude Lévi-Strauss), our ideologies (Louis Althusser), our literary endeavours (Roland Barthes), and even our unconscious (Jacques Lacan) are subject to largely unconscious rules and codes that precede and guide our conscious actions. Because of its emphasis on formal structure over content (the abstract and universal over the concrete and particular), as well as its relative discounting of individual creativity, it was considered antithetical to *humanism* in general and to existentialism in particular.

temporality, ekstatic: Developed by Heidegger, adapted by Sartre and others, but anticipated by Kierkegaard, this refers to the threefold dimension of lived time as distinct from quantitative 'clock' time, namely the past as 'thrownness' or facticity, the future as 'projection' or ekstasis, and the present as 'fallenness' or immersion in the average everyday. It elaborates the existentialist view that we are fundamentallytime-bound but emphasizes the dimension of the future as possibility and, above all, our most proper possibility, our being-unto-death.

Index

Existentialism

Existentialism